We Were the MORRIS ORPHANS

4 BROTHERS, 5 SISTERS & ME

KATHI MORRIS

Post Hill PRESS

A POST HILL PRESS BOOK
ISBN: 978-1-63758-126-1
ISBN (eBook): 978-1-63758-127-8

Post Hill Press
New York • Nashville
posthillpress.com

Published in the United States of America
1 2 3 4 5 6 7 8 9 10

To my parents Robert Gene and Joyce Angela Morris
Your names will live forever on these pages and
in the hearts and souls of your children
In Memory of CJ Collins

Table of Contents

Part Two
MY SIBLINGS' AND PARENTS' STORIES

It is not my intent to defame anyone; rather, to tell my truth and that of my siblings.

Introduction

You might remember me from my fifteen minutes of fame.

On July 2, 1968, a drunk driver killed my parents, orphaning us ten children—aged three to seventeen. We lived in Madera, a small rural town in California where everybody knew everybody. Our parents left us with strong family values but little more. With no estate or relatives willing to adopt us, we became wards of the court.

Our plea to not be separated prompted the tight-knit Madera community to establish a trust fund with Bank of America to "Keep the 10 Morris Orphans Together." While donations trickled in at a slow and steady pace, the *Madera Tribune* reported daily on the fund's status.

Everything changed when *CBS Evening News* aired our plight on national television. Articles titled "Morris Case Familiar in all Parts of the Country" and "10 Orphans Seek to Stay as Family" were reported in newspapers worldwide. Fueled by the publicity, the trust fund skyrocketed. Previously disinterested relatives engaged in a custody battle while offers to adopt us poured in from kindhearted strangers.

On August 28, 1968, a judge, one solitary man, decided our fate, awarding custody of the ten of us to our aunt. When *CBS Evening News with Walter Cronkite* announced that we would remain together, the world rejoiced. Little did they know for two months leading to that decision, inept and calloused professionals and money-hungry, fame-seeking adults flamed our pain. Or that within months of that decision, we were separated, sent to foster homes, and abused.

Throughout my life, upon hearing parts of my life story, friends and strangers alike would say, "You should write a book!" My response was always, "Why? Who would want to read it? Everybody has a story." The common reply was, "Yes, but not like yours!" I ignored the idea until I heard a sermon at Mass. "Each of you has God-given gifts," said the priest. "When you die, God will hold you accountable for them. What is your gift?"

Struck by the gravity of his words, I thought, *hmmm...what is my gift? Writing? Everyone says they enjoy reading my cards and letters.* At that moment, I flashed on the countless number of people who had told me to write a book and how I had dismissed them.

I love the movie *The Wizard of Oz*. In the beginning, Dorothy asks the Munchkins how to find the Land of Oz. In either a high-pitched or low-pitched voice, they instruct her to "Follow the yellow brick road!" Suddenly, I had a visual of exactly that—only the Munchkins were all the people who had said, "You should write a book!"

As I sat in church reflecting, it became clear that telling my story was no longer a choice. I had an *obligation*, commissioned by God.

My story begins with a tragic night in 1968. I spent years reliving my past, researching documents, and conducting interviews to record details as accurately as possible. I found myself often recanting through the memory or perception of a wounded teenager. Most of the adults who contributed to my suffering have died. Strengthened and fortified by years of adversity, I forgave them or moved past the pain long ago, but the memories live on. Some in my yesterday. Some in my today.

I am the oldest of the ten Morris orphans. This is my story. This is *our* story.

Part One

MY STORY

Chapter 1

THE FIRST
FIFTEEN MINUTES

Tuesday, July 2, 1968, was another triple-digit scorcher in Madera—a tiny farmland town in central California. The screen door served as our air conditioner, allowing me a full view of the advancing policeman. Dusk provided me with enough fading sunlight to observe the cop's long strides slow to a cautious trudge as he approached our home.

My nine siblings and I were watching *The Jerry Lewis Show* on the black and white television tucked in the corner beside the front door. When the young officer peered through the screen, his subdued expression changed to bewilderment. Gawking at him were ten kids laying across the tattered furniture and thin worn carpet. Years later, I understood his look was not of bewilderment, but rather, anguished distress. Sent on a mission, he could not know the gravity of what awaited him. His last step must have propelled him into his worst nightmare. I was minutes away from disintegrating into mine.

At seventeen, I was the oldest and in charge when my parents were away. Questions churned in my mind as I crossed the living room to greet him. *Why is a cop here? Did one of us do something wrong? Did Mom and Dad forget to pay a bill? Is he going to take them to jail?*

I did not know if my parents paid bills on time, but I knew money was tight. My dad managed Kaser Shoes, a small store in downtown Madera, and my mother cooked for the nuns at Saint Joachim's Convent. For as long as I could remember, my parents struggled to make ends meet; still, they kept adult matters from us kids. Unable to arrive at a plausible explanation as to why a cop would come to our home, I decided in those few moments that he came for an unpaid bill.

Through the screen door, he asked, "Are your parents home?"

"No, they went to Fresno a couple of hours ago."

"What are their names?"

"Bob and Joyce Morris."

Scanning our small living room, he asked, "Are all of these your brothers and sisters?"

"Yes," I assured him.

"How many are there?"

"Ten."

Rubbing the back of his neck, he asked, "Are you the oldest?"

"Yes."

"How old are you?"

"I'm seventeen." *Why is he asking all these questions?*

"Do you have any other relatives in town?"

"No."

"Where do your nearest relatives live?"

"My grandparents live in Fresno."

Moving his head from side to side, he examined the room a second time. "Wait here," he said, then stepped off the cement landing and hurried to his patrol car parked in front of the house.

When he was out of earshot, I turned toward my brothers and sisters and asked in a hushed voice, "Did any of you break a window or something?" Each eyeballed the other to see who the culprit might be. Shaking their heads, they returned their gaze to me. "So, none of you have any idea why he's here?"

Judy and Carole whispered, "No, Kathi!"

Robert and Mike promised in unison, "I swear to you!"

We continued to deliberate until the car door slammed, and I heard the click of his shoes on the cement walkway. Reaching the doorstep, he waved his hand, motioning for me. "I need you to step outside…alone." Swallowing hard, I felt the first wave of nervousness wash over me. *Why is he telling me to come out by myself? I have never been in trouble.*

I fumbled to unlatch the silver hook on the worn wooden frame of the screen door. Once outside, I felt the rough pavement warm my bare feet. I glanced up and down the streets, looking for any sign of life. The neighborhood eerily devoid of cars and people added to my anxiety. Following the cop to the sidewalk, I looked back at our dimly lit house and saw my siblings in the bedrooms on either side of the living room, crouched under the window ledge, their eyes barely visible through the dark screens.

There we stood, the cop and I, in silence. Since I was shy, obedient, and respectful, I waited for him to speak while he kept his gaze toward the ground. When he raised his head and his eyes met mine, he looked away—as if startled—and twisted his body in every direction but mine. Toward the sidewalk, our boxy white house, the night sky, everywhere but me. *Why won't he say anything? Why won't he look at me?* After several minutes it became clear that if I wanted answers, I would have to ask questions. The agony of waiting for him to speak eclipsed my reluctance to question an authority figure.

"Is something wrong?" My words were barely audible.

"Yes." Silence.

"Are you here because my parents didn't pay a bill?"

"No." Using the back of his hand, he wiped the sweat from his brow.

"Are you here because one of us kids did something wrong?"

"No." He rotated his head as if he could not bear to see my face in front of him.

No? What else could it be? I don't know what more to ask. Rubbing my clammy hands on my cutoffs and twisting my long auburn hair, I continued to wrestle with reasons a cop would come to our house. Labored silence turned to one, two, three minutes when suddenly I made the connection. *Mom and Dad drove away a couple of hours ago!* Surging with panic, I moved in front of him to make him look at me. My voice trembling as I pleaded, "Were my parents in an accident?"

With a pained look, he nodded.

Oh my God, no! My pulse raced. I was desperate for answers and needed him to talk to me. "Did someone get hurt?"

"Yes."

"Who? My mom?" He nodded. "What about my dad?" Another nod. With each nod, my chest tightened as I struggled to breathe. "Did they break an arm or a leg? Which hospital are they in?"

Pivoting, the officer focused on the house. I'm sure he saw my siblings' frightened eyes through the windows.

"They're not in a hospital. It's pretty bad."

Fueled with adrenaline, perplexed by his answers, I struggled to make sense of it all. *How can that be? They were in an accident. It's pretty bad... but they're not in a hospital? Then where are they?* A split second later, the entire world vanished with an inconceivable thought. All that remained was the cop's face suspended in a black vortex. *No, I told myself. It's too scary to ask him that.* Every muscle in my body tightened, like bracing for the blast of a twelve-gauge shotgun, when I asked, "They're not dead, are they?" The officer's body visibly slumped as he delivered his final nod.

"No! No! No! You are lying to me! You are wrong! Are you sure it's my mom and dad?" I searched his face for signs of a mistake. Instead, he stoically and methodically recited the message he was sent to deliver.

"There was an accident on Highway 99. A man and woman were killed by a drunk driver. They are identified as Robert Morris and a woman supposedly his spouse."

Words seared in my memory, branded for eternity.

It took fifteen excruciating minutes to extract from the cop that my parents were dead. A blur for me after hearing his words, my sisters said I ran in circles and jumped across the lawn. I don't remember. What I do recall are the unimaginable words *my mom and my dad are dead. Both of them are dead. They are not coming home*, firing through my mind. I pushed the words away to breathe, but they battled back, exploding like hand grenades, twisting every fiber of my mind and body. Unable to absorb the words, let alone the reality, the agony of that moment has never left me.

As devastating as that night was, my nightmare was just beginning.

Chapter 2

OUT INTO
THE EMPTY

The officer told me to go into the house and call my grandparents. When I opened the screen door, my siblings ran from the bedrooms and into my arms. Judy, Linda, Carole, Theresa, Roberta, Robert, Mike, Jeff, Eddie, and me, all orphaned in an instant.

The house phone—in the bedroom directly off the living room—required walking past Dad's hunter green upholstered chair, ripe with the scent of his Pall Mall cigarettes. The smell reminded me of my father and sent me into another round of crying. I dialed the black rotary phone, and when Grandma answered, I sobbed, "Grandma! Mom and Dad are dead!"

"What? Who is this?"

"Grandma! It's me! Kathi!"

"Kathi, who?"

She knows who this is! Why is she acting like she doesn't recognize my voice? "Grandma! It's Kathi! Your granddaughter!"

"Oh! Kathi! What are you saying?"

"Grandma! Mom and Dad are dead!"

"Are you on drugs?"

I didn't do drugs. My grandmother's baseless question added to the feeling that I had fallen into the Twilight Zone. Nothing felt real. Frustrated, I yelled, "Grandma! No! A cop is here! He came to the house and told us Mom and Dad were killed in a car accident!"

"I don't understand what you are saying!"

Exasperated, I handed the phone to the police officer. "You tell her! She doesn't believe me!"

At least thirty minutes had passed since the cop arrived. The first fifteen with me, trying to extract from him that my parents were killed. The following fifteen were with my grandmother—trying to convince her that her thirty-five-year-old daughter and thirty-nine-year-old son-in-law were dead.

Life as I knew it had ended. *What do I do now? We're all alone.* My wide-eyed siblings, fear etched on their pale faces, looked as lost as me.

Judy, sixteen, the pretty and popular sister, had thick chestnut brown hair and brown eyes. Her clear olive skin favored our dad and his Portuguese side of the family. She was a pep girl, artistically inclined, and infinitely more conservative than I. She was also Mom's favorite. That fact played a significant role with the two of us mixing like oil and water.

Linda, fifteen, freckled, with short light brown hair and hazel eyes, was feisty, headstrong, and dramatic. Cast appropriately as Calamity Jane in a high school play, she walked around half-cocked and ready to fight.

Carole, fourteen, with brown eyes and thin brown hair, was easy-going, fun-loving, and social. She had the most friends. Athletic, she could run like the wind and outrun all the neighborhood boys. She and Linda had similar builds and facial features. When we asked people to guess who the twins were, without fail, they chose the two of them.

Theresa, twelve, was a retiring demure beauty with short, thick, wavy blond hair and blue eyes. She once modeled for Kinney Shoes. An elegant and classy introvert. Had she not been so pretty, she would have been lost in the shadows with her quiet and sweet demeanor.

We five oldest girls comprised the big kids.

The eleven-year-old fraternal twins, Robert and Roberta, were the oldest of the little kids. Roberta, older than Robert by nineteen minutes, had thick short brown hair, large brown eyes, and pixie features. Born with a flat head because her eight-pound brother sat on top of it, she was the only child who pushed Mom to therapy. It drove our mother nuts when she refused to eat anything green or with certain textures. The youngest of us six girls, Roberta often wore hand-me-downs. She struggled to fit in because she was stifled by us older sisters and lumped in with the boys.

Robert, the first boy after six girls, was Dad's pride and joy. He had thick red hair, hazel eyes, and wore glasses. He had common sense and would go with the flow. I resented him because I fancied myself as Dad's favorite until Robert was born.

Michael, ten, intelligent, cocky, and cute, had hazel eyes framed with thick sandy blond hair combed to the side, surfer style. Athletic and solid as a rock, he used his small stature to charm all the girls. He had a mind of his own and could be hard to handle.

Jeffrey, eight, was the sweet, easy-going, loveable brother with thick wavy blond hair and blue eyes. He was an average student with an ever-ready smile. Friendly and soft-spoken by nature, Robert often enlisted him to gang up on Mike.

The youngest, Edward, three, had big brown eyes, soft blond hair, and a sweet disposition. Mom had a hysterectomy after his birth and spoiled him rotten because he was her last child. He was probably the easiest for our parents to raise because, by then, there were six older girls to help care for him.

I was the surrogate mother—forced into the role when Mom periodically worked. My brothers and sister obeyed me as much as they did our parents. So, while the police officer continued to reason with my grandmother, I gave orders. "Linda! Go tell Jane what happened!" Jane, Mom's best friend from high school, lived around the corner. "Carole! Go tell Mrs. Carter." She lived across the street and was a good friend of our mother's. Judy and I both called our boyfriends.

Roberta sat rocking baby Eddie, who was too young to understand. His chubby cheeks were wet with tears because all his siblings were crying. As I stroked his silky hair, I sorted through the rubble of my shattered heart, unable to find words to comfort him. *Eddie will never know how much his mommy and daddy loved him.*

As word spread, it did not take long for droves of neighbors, friends, and relatives to fill our home. A priest from St. Joachim's Catholic Church rushed over, as well as a doctor. The doctor asked each of us questions to assess who needed a tranquilizer. We rarely took pills in our family, so when he questioned me, I asked, "What is it for?"

"It's to help calm you," he replied.

"No, thank you. I think I'm okay." I refused the pill and later wished he had insisted because that evening became the first of many sleepless nights.

As the hours grew long, I sat on the sofa nearest the front door with the boys at my side. Judy sat across from me in Dad's chair, her face twisted in terror, rocking back and forth. Her arms were wrapped tightly around a statue of the Virgin Mary that she had taken from our parent's bedroom. The figure sat proudly on our parent's dresser and meant a lot to our mother. When Judy looked up and our eyes met, it was as if our spirits acknowledged the same fear and helplessness.

I scanned the living room and realized I didn't recognize most of the people. They stood shoulder to shoulder, their backs against the walls, tears streaming down their faces.

The night ended the same way it began—adults standing across from me, in silence.

Chapter 3

VIOLETS ARE BLUE

I spent the day of the accident with my boyfriend, Richard—a sexy Italian with lush black hair and bedroom eyes. We cruised around Madera in his red Chevy Corvair and made a pit stop at the Big Top Drive-in for a cherry lime rickey, then headed out to rollercoaster hills for cheap thrills. Rising from the expansive flatlands, with acres of yellow wildflowers, stretched a long country road with low dips and high crests where it was easy to bottom out at high speeds. Something only wild teenagers would think of doing—and we did.

Instructed to return by 6:00 p.m., we parked directly across the street from the front of our white corner house trimmed in yellow. A light blue 1961 Mercury four door sedan sat on the road running adjacent to our property. On loan for a week, my parents were driving that car when they were killed.

I was staring at our home when the front door opened. Dad stepped out in his brown and white striped short-sleeved shirt and khaki pants. He kept a quick pace as he crossed the lawn to open the passenger door of the car. Mom, with her sandy blond hair, bouffant style, and blue, knee-length shift, strolled behind him. Slow enough to debate whether I should bolt out of the car and ask to tag along. I decided against it and lived to regret that decision. Death would have been preferable to the pain, loneliness, and rejection of the ensuing years.

Two hours later, they were dead.

That night, sleep was fleeting as I wrestled with my mind's eye. Words and images tormented me all night. My parents crossing the lawn to the car. The cop at the door. His lips pushing out words exploding like the detonation of a nuclear bomb, leaving nothing behind but my hemorrhaging heart. The swells of panic, twisted stomach, and constricted breathing were new and debilitating feelings that I wanted nothing to do with.

To steal a few minutes of sleep, I pretended that it did not happen. *Mom and Dad are coming home. They are on vacation, and any minute they will walk through the front door.* I dozed off for a few minutes before being startled awake again to my nightmarish reality.

⤳

It is the following morning— my first morning without parents. I am seventeen years old, and today I do not have my mom or dad. I did yesterday, but today, my parents are dead.

The morning sun brought with it a disconnected and unfamiliar world. A constant stream of people stopped by. Some pressed money into my grandmother's hands while many more delivered food. Canned goods, casseroles, and desserts filled every room of the house, including the living room and our parents' bedroom. I looked around and thought, *where were all these people when my parents were struggling to feed us?*

There were periods of our life when food was scarce. On occasion, dinner consisted of a wedge of lettuce smeared with mayonnaise. We collected Pepsi bottles and exchanged them for a loaf of bread. Junk food was out of the question because we had just enough money for three meals and school lunches. For a few months, we survived on government surplus food. Mom went to a food distribution center and returned with a cardboard box filled with a block of pasteurized cheese, powdered milk, and canned meat mimicking Spam. We never went hungry, but we were not allowed—nor did it occur to us—to eat between meals. That day, surrounded by enough food to feed the entire town, I had no appetite.

My maternal grandparents, Bolis and Violet Lachawicz, sixty-one, and my Aunt Mary, seventeen and their youngest child, stayed with us the night of the accident. Grandma Lachawicz was the grandmother I called to tell our parents were killed. At seventeen, naïve and overcome with grief, it did not occur to me that they, too, were distraught. They lost their oldest daughter, and Aunt Mary lost her only sister. In addition, they had the burden of comforting and caring for the ten of us. I can only now imagine their pain.

My paternal grandmother, Mollie Morris, sixty-one, arrived the day after the accident. Her husband, my grandfather Angelo, died ten years earlier at fifty-two with his third heart attack. My father, twenty-nine at the time of his father's death, attended the funeral without us. When he returned, he was inconsolable for a week. Dad sat on the front doorstep, weeping with his head cradled in his hands. I had never seen him cry. As an impressionable seven-year-old—and a Daddy's girl at that—watching him grieve left an indelible mark. To break my hero, I decided that death and funerals must be something on this side of hell.

Ten years later, I was facing my first funeral—for both my mom and my dad.

A Catholic funeral—Rosary, Mass, and a Catholic cemetery—was never in question. My mother and the ten of us were cradle Catholics, meaning we were baptized and raised in the Catholic faith. My father was raised Lutheran and converted to Catholicism after he married my mother. The ten of us attended Catechism and Mass our entire lives.

Funerals in the 1960s were held within three days of a death, which required immediate action. As the oldest, my grandparents invited me to go with them and Aunt Mary to Jay's Chapel to make funeral arrangements. A daunting task for a sheltered seventeen-year-old in a state of shock. Harder, still, because my grandparents only had to choose one coffin—for their daughter. I had to choose two. One for my mom and one for my dad.

The four of us piled into my grandparents' blue Malibu. My grandfather drove while my grandmother sat next to him, reading the local newspaper, the *Madera Tribune*. She read silently, then turned and handed the paper to me in the backseat. I grabbed it and opened it to the front page. I read the headline, "Madera Couple, Parents of 10 Children, Killed," and instantly broke into uncontrollable sobbing. I cried the night before, but not like that. Reading it in print somehow made it more real. The cries from a guttural pain erupting from the depths of my soul lasted until we arrived at the funeral home. The article read:

Ten Madera children were orphaned after a grinding, five-car wrong-way crash near Fresno Tuesday night snuffed out the lives of their parents Robert G Morris, 39, and his wife Joyce, 35. The young couple is survived by a closely-knit family ranging in ages from 3-17 who vow, "We will stick together."

A trust fund this morning was established by the grandparents of the children to prevent the youngsters from having to be separated. The trust will be administered by Mrs. Morris's father, Bolis Lachawicz, Morris' Mother, Mrs. Mollie Morris, and Mrs. Evelyn Massetti, a close friend of the family who live at 921 W. Sixth St. Donations to it can be made by addressing contributions to the Morris Family Trust Fund, Bank of America, Madera.

Morris, manager of Kaser's Shoes, came here from Fresno three years ago.

The Porterville driver whose wrong-way driving caused the freeway pileup in which the Morrises were killed was booked into the Fresno County Jail late Tuesday on a felony drunk driving charge. The Highway Patrol identified Clifford A. Salmon, 61, as the driver of the car headed north in the southbound lanes of Highway 99 near the Ashlan Avenue turnoff in Fresno, triggering a five-car crash about 8 last night. A Chowchilla woman, Rudy Hale, 60, was a passenger in Salmon's car. Both she and Salmon were listed as suffering minor injuries.

I placed the paper on my lap and lifted my eyes to the nape of my grandfather's leathered neck, creased with time. *The man that killed Mom and Dad is the same age as Grandpa!*

Reading on, I saw:

> The CHP said that the Morris vehicle rammed into the three other cars after the initial collision with Salmon's car. A passenger in one of the other cars, Jeannette Miller, 33, Walnut, suffered multiple injuries in the crash and was hospitalized in Fresno.
>
> Morris and his wife were testing out a car, owned by a Fresno woman when the crash occurred. They had intended to purchase the vehicle.
>
> All of the children were at home when the police and St. Joachim priests broke the grim news to them. The children and their ages: Edward, 3; Jeffrey, 8; Michael, 10; Robert and Roberta, twins, 11; Theresa, 12; Carole, 14; Linda, 15; Judy, 16; and Kathleen (sic), 17. The younger children attend St. Joachim's while the others are Madera High School pupils. "We were all close," said pretty, dark-haired Judy today through tear-filled eyes. "That is why we all want to stay together." She plans on majoring in art at Fresno State College.

I looked out the window and thought about the man, Clifford Salmon, and how he would react. *He will feel bad when he sobers up and realizes he killed the parents of ten kids.* The article continued:

The entire family participated in church-related programs. Morris was head of the St. Joachim's group of Confraternity of Catholic Doctrine teachers who give religious instruction to youngsters attending public schools. His wife and older children also helped in this endeavor. Morris was a member of the Madera Action Committee and had served as Chairman of the Decency Petition campaign.

While the children are holding up bravely through the ordeal, scores of friends have brought the family piles of food. Relatives from Fresno and the Bay Area are also here.

Rosary will be Thursday night at 8 in St. Joachim's Church with funeral Mass Friday at the church at 9:30 a.m. Burial will be in Calvary cemetery. Jay's Funeral Home is handling arrangements.

Besides the children, Morris is survived by his mother Mollie Morris of Concord; sisters Gloria Graves, Concord; Eleanor Azevedo, Pittsburg; Sandra Touchstone, Concord; a brother, Butch Morris of Richmond; great-grandparents, Mr. and Mrs. Pedro Morris of Hayward. Mrs. Morris also is survived by her parents, Mr. and Mrs. Bolis Lachawicz of Fresno; brothers Eugene P. Lachawicz of Fresno and Steven B. Lachawicz of New Jersey, and Mary V of Fresno.

I stared at the headlines. *I'm in a nightmare. I can't believe any of this is real.* It didn't matter that my grandparents and aunt were in the car. I felt alone. So incredibly alone.

Grandpa parked in front of Jay's Chapel, turned his head toward Mary and me in the back seat, and gave us a look that said, "Let's go," without saying a word. Any other day he would have turned with a smile and said in his Chicago accent, "C'mon, you little shootusses!" and we would laugh.

But not today.

I took in a deep breath, opened the car door, and stepped into the blazing sunlight. My stomach rolled as I turned to look at the building. The pitched roof, brick façade, and plate glass windows looked non-threatening, which helped relieve some anxiety. Still, I kept a slow pace behind my grandparents.

Grandpa, stocky, his once jet-black hair faded to grey, in a beige dress shirt, deep brown slacks, and olive-green cardigan reached the door first. Grandma, 5'2" with bouffant-style brown hair, smoothed the wrinkles on her sleeveless floral dress as she stepped inside. Mary and I followed behind.

The funeral director was wearing a black suit and waiting in the lobby. Extending his hand to Grandpa, he said, "Hello, my name is Robert Jay. I want to offer my sincere condolences for your loss."

"Thank you. This is my wife, Violet, our daughter Mary, and our oldest granddaughter Kathi."

Robert opened his arms to hug me. "I'm so sorry, Kathi. I am here to help you and your grandparents as best I can." His voice was soft and comforting.

"Thank you. Can you tell me where the restroom is?"

Placing one hand on my back, he used the other to point. "It's that way. Take your time. We will be waiting for you in my office down the hall."

Inside the tiled restroom, I headed straight for the oval-shaped mirror hanging above the porcelain sink. *Jeez, Mary…why didn't you tell me how bad I looked?* Mary and I were both self-conscious teenagers who never left the house without perfect hair and makeup. Foundation. Blush. Brown eyeshadow with white highlights. Perfectly drawn black eyeliner. And most important, loads of black mascara.

Staring at me was a masked bandit raccoon with dark streaks running down its cheeks. I grabbed some paper towels, slathered them with soap and water, and removed all traces of my tear-filled journey. Satisfied that no makeup looked better than the state of my arrival, I pushed the door open and headed down the hall, in the direction of their voices. The floral scent of the soap covering my face and invading my nose diverted my thoughts, if only for a second.

Inside the office, I settled into the tufted armchair next to Aunt Mary. I feigned listening as the adults discussed details. Limousines. Police motorcade. Holy cards. Like white noise, none of it interested me until Robert stood up and announced, "Let's move to the next room to select the caskets." I know my face paled.

Everyone stood up and followed the director, single file, with me at the tail end. When I rounded the corner, my knees buckled like an elevator dropping to the ground. Coffins filled every inch of space, with many of them double stacked. I looked around the room and thought *there are so many of them! Look at those made of wood… and these pink and blue ones.* As we made our way to the back of the room, I noticed more details—like the ornate carvings, gilded handles, and white satin interiors. My mind continued to churn. *Why on earth do* dead people need so many frills? They can't see the pretty colors or feel the fluffy padding. It was all so curious to me.

After surveying them all, Grandma turned to me and asked, "What do you think, Kathi?"

"Grandma, Mom always said she wanted to be buried in a pine box in the backyard."

A solemn acknowledgment washed over Grandma's face as her eyes filled with tears. Shifting her stance, she tilted her head and said to the director, "Please show us your least expensive caskets."

"Follow me," he said, and led us to a simple coffin. It might have been one level up from a pine box. I don't remember because the entire process seemed bizarre to me. Complying with Mom's request would have been a lot less taxing on my nerves because after choosing their coffins, I learned that we still weren't done. Robert led us back to his office to discuss their burial clothes.

My father, a manager for shoe stores most of my life, owned several suits. To bury him in one of them was a quick and easy decision. However, my mother was a different story. My mother's wardrobe consisted of practical clothing—not much at that. She did not own a formal dress; certainly, not one befitting a funeral attended by hundreds of people. Our eyes darted from one to the other as reality sank in. The lines in Grandma's forehead creased as she turned to Grandpa. "Pa, I think we need to buy something for Joyce."

Robert said, "I may be able to help you. We keep some clothing available for purchase. You might find something you like. Follow me."

The funeral director led us to another room and opened a closet door. "Please, take a look." Inside were several dresses of varying lengths, colors, and styles.

Grandma coaxed Grandpa, "You choose." I stood back and watched his weathered hand, covered with age spots and broken blood vessels, push one dress on the rod, then the next, and grappled with the why. *Why is something buried in the ground and never seen again so important?* Grandma clung to Grandpa's arm as if to steady herself while his hands shook in an odd trembling rhythm. And when he stopped, choked up, and pulled out a dress, I understood the why. A single tear rolled down his cheek as he turned to show us his little girl's burial dress. It was more beautiful than anything she had ever owned as our mother.

Mom, at the tender age of thirty-five, was buried in a soft, chiffon dress.

It was violet—her favorite color.

It was violet—the name of her mother.

Madera Couple, Parents Of 10 Children, Killed

MADERA *Daily* TRIBUNE

" THE ONLY DAILY NEWSPAPER IN PROSPEROUS MADERA COUNTY — HEART OF THE SAN JOAQUIN VALLEY "

Continuing The Madera Daily News-Tribune

:Weather:
FAIR
High 100 - 106

MADERA, CALIF., WEDNESDAY, JULY 3, 1963

July 3 Headline: Madera Couple Killed

Chapter 4

THE FINAL ACT

When we were growing up, unbridled excitement filled the Fourth of July. Mom had a knack for making every holiday special. Dad, a kid at heart, loved his annual opportunity to play with pyrotechnics. Between the two of them, we knew it was a day guaranteed to tickle all our senses.

Mom worked tirelessly in the kitchen, preparing food for our picnic. She filled our large yellow Tupperware bowl with potato salad and sprinkled crimson paprika across the top. She boiled golden corn on the cob and cut the sweet red watermelon into triangles. Her coveted peach cobbler made with Bisquick and fresh peaches could have won a blue ribbon at a county fair.

We kids would grab a slice of watermelon, head to the back yard, and challenge each other to see who could spit the black seeds the farthest; meanwhile, Dad fired up the briquets in his black Weber barbecue. He grilled hot dogs, juicy hamburgers topped with a slice of

American cheese, and toasted the buns. I loved the smell of barbecue wafting in the summer breeze.

When the picnic ended, the setting sun whipped us into a frenzy. Mom spread a checkered quilt on the uneven lawn. Dad fetched the main attraction: The Red Devil Family Assortment of Fireworks. Squeals of delight erupted when he appeared with the box—all of us clamoring to see its contents. Seventy-five pieces cost a whopping $6.95 with a Star-Spangled Salute tossed in for free.

When the sun finally set, Dad lit a string of firecrackers. The loud popping, like gunfire, drove Mom insane. "Bob! Is that really necessary?" Her annoyance was met with Dad's mischievous grin.

"Maybe you'll like these better," he teased. The boys beaming smiles and giggles just egged him on. He dropped to his knees and placed tiny pellets, called Black Snakes, on the sidewalk while we kids formed a circle around him. Using the sidewalk to light a match, he lit one pellet and then another. The good snakes would start growing at once. Smoking, twisting, and turning—sometimes straight up. They left a black trail of ash on the pavement and happiness in their wake. Black Snakes were the next best thing to firecrackers in Dad's book.

Once the boys finished playing on the ground, Dad grabbed a bucket and hose while we settled in for the show. The high-pitched scream of Piccolo Pete filled the sizzling summer night while cones shot glimmering gold high into the air, tendrils trailing gently to the ground. Fountains crackled and bathed the sky with a spectacular shower of green or red. The pinwheel nailed to a tree whistled as it spun and emitted bright silver rays. Sulfur filled our nostrils and stung our eyes, but we didn't care.

Sparklers, my favorite, hissed and spewed twinkling stars while I carved the letters of my name against the night's dark backdrop. Saved for last, they signaled the end of the show…much like July 4, 1968, when we saw our parents for the last time.

⌣

My parents died on Tuesday. Wednesday, we made funeral arrangements. The viewing and Rosary were on Thursday, the Fourth of July. Unlike the Fourth of July in years past, none of us looked forward to that night.

All of us were familiar with saying the Rosary. We recited it our entire lives. If we couldn't fall asleep and cried out to Mom, she'd yell, "Say the Rosary!" Most of the time, it worked with the repetitive chanting of fifty Hail Mary's—like counting sheep. When we stayed with Grandma Lachawicz, we said the Rosary before going to bed. I hated every boring minute of that.

What we were not familiar with was the viewing. The closest we'd come to seeing dead bodies was watching Westerns on television. I was incredibly nervous because the previous day, I overheard a conversation between my grandparents. The funeral home called and asked for Grandma Morris. They advised a closed casket for Dad because—despite their best effort—they were unable to restore him to an acceptable state. Our father had severe injuries because he had been ejected from the car and run over. The funeral home felt his disfigurement would upset the family, especially us kids. Grandma Morris, despite their recommendation, insisted on an open casket.

When Grandma Morris hung up with the funeral home, Grandpa Lachawicz said, "Mollie, I understand you want Bob's casket open, but I think you need to consider their advice."

"It's my son! I don't want a closed casket!" Grandma snapped. Usually gentle and soft-spoken, her raised voice and curt response surprised me. Her hand trembled as she lifted her menthol cigarette to her pursed lips.

"I'll go to Jay's and let you know what I think," Grandpa offered.

Grandma's glare and mumbling as she scrambled out of the living room left no doubt that she intended to stand her ground.

My grandfather was more than qualified to supply an opinion. He had spent thirty-one years in the funeral business. His father opened the Stephen D. Lachawicz funeral home in 1916, in Chicago, Illinois, when Grandpa was nine years old. We grew up listening to stories about living above the funeral parlor, embalming, and preparing bodies for burial.

I knew things were bad when Grandpa returned from Jay's Chapel with downcast eyes and a pained look marring his face. He tried his best to convince Grandma of a closed casket, but she refused to change her mind.

The following day, the ten of us piled into several of our relatives' cars for the short trip to the church for the viewing and Rosary. St. Joachim's, a church we attended every Sunday, had a vibrant mosaic of Jesus, floor to ceiling, on the wall behind the altar. A huge wooden cross suspended from the ceiling hung in front of the mosaic. Beams ran the length of the cathedral. Stained glass windows and the Stations of the Cross adorned the walls.

Fear weighed heavy as we shuffled stoically into the pews like wooden puppets, the sound of our shoes clapping against the cold stone floor. I followed Grandma Lachawicz to the first pew while Carole, carrying Eddie, trailed behind me.

"Let Eddie sit back here," whispered Roberta.

"No, honey, he needs to sit with me!" Grandma Lachawicz said in a commanding voice.

Although I noticed the two wooden caskets when we entered the church, it wasn't until we settled in that I allowed myself to study them. Both rested at the base of the altar and were placed end to end. The longer I stared at them, the more nervous I became. Dread rose from the pit of my stomach. I battled polarized thoughts of finally getting to see my parents again and suffocating anxiety over what they looked like. My parents were my rock. My protectors. The captains and navigators of my life. Left with no instructions on how to continue without them, I pretended they were still alive. In minutes, I would have proof that they weren't.

Grandma Lachawicz, the first to stand, urged me to rise. Like a lamb led to slaughter, I followed, trying to stay calm as my heart hammered out of my chest. The casket nearest to us had my mother in it. As we inched forward, I felt lightheaded and weak-kneed. *What will she look like? Will she be all white? Will she have dark circles around her eyes?*

Grandma, in front of me and carrying Eddie, partially blocked my view. I strained to see around her and noticed Mom's pretty dress and hands—one placed on top of the other, clasping a white rosary. When my grandmother moved, I took the final step towards the casket and blew out some anxiety.

It wasn't as bad as I imagined. Mom looked like she was sleeping. More accurately, she looked like a version of herself sleeping. Her hair was styled differently, and she wasn't wearing her glasses. Her makeup was different—the blue eyeshadow and pink lipstick were something she never wore. That bothered me because I wanted to see her as I remembered her. Grandma had told me that when her mother died, she was smiling and looked at peace. Mom was not smiling. She did not look peaceful. The longer I studied her, the more anxious I became because it looked like she could open her eyes and sit up.

Suddenly my grandmother reached inside the casket and caressed Mom's hand. It took me aback—it was so unexpected. *What is she doing? What does Mom feel like? I don't think I want to know.* Grandma continued to talk to Mom and stroke her hand, then turned to look at me. She motioned her head, as if to say *it's your turn.* My stomach turned somersaults. I hesitated, then reluctantly obeyed, and immediately wished I hadn't. After feeling her cold and spongy flesh, I snapped my hand back as if I'd burnt myself on a hot iron. I'd seen and felt enough and moved on to my father.

As I approached Dad's casket, I expected him, like my mother, to look like a version of himself sleeping. When I took the last step and looked inside, to my horror, I found it was not the case. Grandma should have listened to Grandpa and the funeral home. The guy in the casket was not my father. I searched his face, hair, and hands for something to make me believe it was. My dad, tall and thin, stood 5'11" and weighed one hundred and forty-five pounds. The guy in the casket looked heavy—like he was bloated. Everywhere I looked, he looked swollen. As I studied him, I became more perplexed. *Why is his head tilted to the side? Is that a wig? Is that lipstick? What is going on?*

Soon, Carole and Linda joined me. As soon as she looked inside, Carole scowled. "That does *not* look like Daddy!"

Linda covered her gaping mouth with her hand and exclaimed, "No, it does not!"

I remained by Dad's casket while the rest of my brothers and sisters approached. Each of them recoiled with the same reaction—disbelief and confusion. None of us could identify what, why, or how he looked different. We had no interest in studying him further and spent little time looking at him.

When the viewing was over, we recited the Rosary. For me, it was another exercise of just going through the motions. I could not concentrate or engage in the prayers. I ached for the nightmare to end.

The sun had set when we headed home, passing families gathered for the holiday. The night was filled with the sounds of whistling Piccolo Pete, firecrackers, and colorful fireworks. Sulfur and children's laughter. Reminders of joy-filled days with our parents were replaced with numbing emptiness.

There was no Fourth of July celebration for us Morris orphans. We left our parents lying in coffins at the church and returned home to prepare for the last scene.

⌁

Friday, July 5, 1968

The day of the funeral.

We dressed in our Sunday best and squeezed into two white limousines. The luxurious cars were a treat and welcome reprieve. Once we settled in, I looked around at my brothers and sisters, grinning with genuine smiles for the first time in days.

"This is pretty cool," ten-year-old Mike chuckled.

"Yeah, look at this," eight-year-old Jeff said as he bounced on the plush seat.

Grandma gave them the same look she gave us at Mass when it was time to be reverent.

When we arrived at St Joachim's, the parking lot was full and cars lined the streets. When we entered the church, I was shocked by the number of people in the pews, aisles, and foyer. As we made our way up the aisle, my attention turned from the multitude of people to the two caskets placed side by side at the front of the church. The United States flag draped over my dad's casket honored his service as a Marine.

Mass was a blur, then and now, because I was consumed with fear. I do not remember the eulogy, who spoke, or where we sat. My focus remained on my parents and the finality of that day when they would become one with the earth. All traces of them erased forever. I desperately clung to every ticking minute and their illusion. No matter that they were encased in a closed box, I envisioned them alive.

When Mass ended, the ten of us marched down the center aisle behind our parent's caskets. I tried my best to avoid looking at the congregation because their tear-stained faces made me feel worse.

When we exited the church, we stood grouped on the church steps and watched in silence as the pallbearers—prominent men from Madera—placed the caskets into the hearse. Our silence continued as we got into the limousines. The funeral procession to Calvary Cemetery, two-and-a-half-miles away, was bumper to bumper with traffic stopped the entire distance.

As we made our way to the open graves, people opened a path and offered condolences. Although I was grateful for their kindness, it was uncomfortable for me to hug or shake hands with so many strangers.

Like the Mass, I remember very little of the service. I do not recall who spoke or what was said. In my mind's eye, I cannot see the caskets or the ten of us sitting at the gravesite.

Acutely aware that time was slipping away, I stayed in my head. As long as my parents were above ground, I could tell myself lies. When the caskets lowered, I had to face the truth. They weren't on vacation.

They would never walk through the front door again. There would never, ever be another Fourth of July with my mom and my dad.

Ill-equipped to deal with reality, I hid in a protective bubble and erased the memory of that day.

Like the final act in a play, the curtain just dropped.

Chapter 5

TRUST FUND

After the funeral, we went home. There was no wake or funeral reception. The ten of us never, ever discussed those four horrific days, beginning with the accident on Tuesday and ending on Friday with the funeral. We returned home without fanfare to carve out a new way of life in a strange new world.

Uncle Steve, our mother's brother, took us to the stock car races at the Madera Speedway that weekend. He wanted to take us back to the days before our living hell when we had innocence sewn into our souls like golden threads.

When we arrived at the raceway, we sprinted from the car to the stadium and found our spots on the aluminum bleachers. The little kids shouted and clapped their hands as the brightly colored cars paraded in front of us and the drivers jockeyed for position. The glaring floodlights, set high on towers, illuminated our view through a haze of cigarette smoke. The hum of a thousand people talking erupted into earsplitting cheers when a booming voice announced the start of the race over the loudspeaker. With the wave of a green flag, burning rubber and exhaust quenched our yearning for a distraction.

An hour into the race, I looked around at the families laughing and stuffing their faces with overpriced hot dogs smeared with mustard. Kids were stepping on everyone's shoes and spilling their sticky soft drinks while their mothers yelled at them to be careful. It made me sad as I thought, *Mom would have yelled at us, too. At least they have a mother.*

Out of nowhere, a sense of impending doom swept over me. I felt sick to my stomach and dizzy and looked at Uncle Steve as if the sight of him would ground me. He was too busy laughing and enjoying the race to notice my struggle to breathe.

I didn't understand why I felt terrible in the middle of a great time. I didn't have tidy, descriptive words like anxiety.

I left the bleachers and walked until I felt better. Like first stage labor pains or an earthquake registering one on the Richter scale, that episode was the calm before the storm. My anxiety gained momentum over the years and eventually took on a life of its own.

After the races, we returned home and found a full front-page editorial in the *Madera Tribune*. The headline read, "Funeral Tribute To Robert Morrises Cites 10 Children As Legacy." Included were two large photos: one inside the church and another of the ten of us in our living room. It read:

> "We must never forget the years God gave us with these people," intoned the Rev. Salvatore Bentivegna this morning at the Mass for Mr. and Mrs. Robert Morris....

Speaking to a crowd of mourners larger than the turnout for the ecumenical service for Sen. Robert F. Kennedy.

The story of the children's resolve to remain together is being told throughout the nation today with articles and pictures sent out by United Press International and requested individually by major newspapers in several cities.

The family has sought no money but established the trust fund in response to requests from friends that they be allowed to help in some way.

As cited in the article, our family had not requested money. However, the day after my parents were killed, Evelyn Massetti, a good friend of my mother's, came to our home to offer her condolences. She and my grandparents sat at the green Formica dining table edged in chrome. I eavesdropped from the adjacent living room.

"People in Madera want to know how they can help," said Mrs. Massetti. She was an English teacher at Madera High School and well known within the small town.

"Many have helped already," Grandma Lachawicz responded. She waved her hand toward the piles of canned food stacked on the hardwood floor and desserts on the buffet. Her heavy eyelids reflected the strain of the previous twenty-four hours. "Look at all this food. We've run out of places to put it."

Grandma Morris reached into the pocket of her cotton housecoat dotted with yellow flowers. Usually stuffed with tissues, Salem cigarettes, and a green Bic lighter, she pulled out a handful of bills.

"Look, I've gotten close to a hundred dollars this morning from total strangers stopping by."

Evelyn continued, leaning in with clasped hands. "I know Bob and Joyce lived paycheck to paycheck."

Grandpa leaned back in his chair and nodded in agreement.

"Are any of you familiar with trust funds?" Evelyn asked. Both grandmothers shook their heads no.

"Can't say that I am," Grandpa answered, scratching the top of his head.

"It's like a savings account managed by a group of people called trustees. Anyone interested in helping the kids could donate money to the fund."

Grandpa, a simple man, said, "That sounds like a great suggestion, but I wouldn't know where to begin with setting one up."

"I can take care of the details," Evelyn responded. "I know an attorney and an executive with Bank of America downtown. I called them before I headed over here. We are willing to draft it today, naming ourselves as trustees, and hit the ground running. All we need are your blessings."

"Consider it blessed," Grandpa said.

The following day, Lester J Gendron, Evelyn Massetti, and the Bank of America National Trust and Savings Association entered a declaration of trust for our use. It read:

> The purpose of this trust is to provide the beneficiaries herein with the means to become educated to the best of the beneficiary's ability and to make available for all of said beneficiaries' funds for extraordinary situations that may not be definitively set forth herein.

Two days later, the Associated Press published our plight in major newspapers across the country. United Press International published it overseas, including the *Pacific Stars and Stripes*, the newspaper read by our soldiers serving in Vietnam. Once our story hit the papers, nobody could have foreseen what happened next. Hundreds of calls from across the nation flooded the *Madera Tribune* and Bank of America. People wanted to know how to send money, adopt, or foster us. Some offered to hand over their homes. A family in the Midwest with nine children said they would buy a bigger house to accommodate us.

As our story spread, television and newspaper reporters descended upon our small farm town for interviews and pictures. As the oldest, I was the spokesperson. Most of the time, the correspondents were kind. But there was one brunette, in her twenties, whose insensitive question threw me into a tailspin.

She and I were standing in our living room near the fireplace. It was a hectic day, with all my siblings and the adults scurrying throughout the house. She pulled out her black microphone and asked me a couple of forgettable questions; but, when she asked, "How does it feel to be an orphan?" I saw red.

How does it feel to be an orphan? What kind of question is that? If looks could kill, she would have joined my parents on the spot. With a steely glare and all the attitude I could muster, I replied, "I am not an orphan! Orphans don't have anyone who cares about them. Look around this house. We are surrounded by family!" And with that, I turned and stormed away. She seemed amused that she got a rise out of me, and I, for the first time, felt the sting of the word *orphan*.

Although the news articles helped the trust fund increase, the turning point was a five-minute broadcast on the *CBS Evening News with Walter Cronkite.* After the segment aired publicizing our plea to stay together, the trust fund skyrocketed.

Initially, the fund increased at a snail's pace. On July 9, the trust fund totaled $2,400. On July 10, $4,000. After the CBS news report on July 12, the fund increased by $5,000 a day. Bank of America hired six women to do nothing but open the stacks of mail. The fund totaled $40,000 by the end of July and topped out at $50,000 by the end of August.

Behind the scenes were the known and unknown—far too many to list them all. Examples are people like the former Mint Director George Gillen, Senior Advisor to the Sumitomo Bank Director in San Francisco. He initiated a fundraising campaign and ran a classified ad in the *San Francisco Chronicle* promoting it.

Central Valley KFRE radio station celebrities Gus Zernial and Al Radka arranged a doubleheader softball contest. Their team, the KFRE No Stars, played against the *Daily Tribune,* followed by a match between Babe Ruth and the American Legion.

A Catholic organization, the Young Men's Institute, held a benefit barbecue and set up an education account. Those of us in high school received $150, and the kids in elementary school $50 per year. Many of those gracious men were pillars of Madera, friends of my parents, and their pallbearers.

Schools got into the act as well. The Jefferson Youth Group from Thomas Jefferson Middle School, where my sister Theresa attended, held a car wash. The Gearlords, a band, composed of my classmates from Madera High School—Ernie Palacio, Dwayne Burns, Dennis Dilbeck (RIP), and Ricky Clymore—held a benefit dance.

Thousands of individuals, organizations, and business owners sent money with touching sympathy cards, from the Citizens Band Radio Group in Fortuna to the Root Beer stand in Palo Alto.

One of the most instantly gratifying gifts was from the Madera County Employees Association and Superintendent of School Classified Employees. They opened a three-hundred-dollar clothing allowance with JC Penney. One would have thought we were in Disneyland as we carried our bounty of school clothes down the escalator, grinning from ear to ear.

All donations were cherished and appreciated; however, the money sent from our military serving in Vietnam was incredibly heartwarming. I had many classmates and a cousin serving at that time and knew firsthand that the money they sent was earned with their blood, sweat, and tears.

⌐

The "Ten Morris Orphans" came with a dowry. A $50,000 trust fund, equivalent to $372,000 in 2020, was security for anyone willing to foster or adopt us. The social security death benefits, $65 per child, was a tidy sum of monthly income. It totaled $7,800 yearly, equivalent to the median annual salary in 1968.

Many wanted to adopt or foster us for all the right reasons. Many others wanted notoriety or access to $50,000 and a year's pay.

We were kids, orphaned, caught in a tornado, trying to find a soft place to land. The money was of no interest to us. We didn't ask for it, we never saw it, and it would not bring back the two things we wanted most: our mom and dad.

Surrounded by uncertainty, we knew only one thing for certain: We were in the spotlight.

July 5, front page, funeral tribute

Funeral Tribute To Robert Morrises Cites 10 Children As Legacy

Madera Tribune, Friday, July 5, 1968 by Charles Dybdal

"We must never forget the years God gave us with these people," intoned the Rev. Salvatore Bentivegna this morning at the Mass for Mr. and Mrs. Robert Morris, killed Tuesday night in a head-on collision. Speaking to a crowd of mourners larger than the turnout for the ecumenical service for Sen. Robert F. Kennedy, Father Bentivegna read from the fourth chapter of St. Paul's letter to the Thessalonians and from the book of John. "In the resurrection, we have been given hope," reminded the priest. "This is what the Morrises taught, and this is what they believed." Many members of the Confraternity of Catholic Doctrine classes which the Morrises taught listened as the Rev. Bentivegna encouraged them to put reason into practice and accept the fact that though the Morrises would be missed, they had begun new life. The Morrises left legacy that few people have left to the world, the priest pointed out. "They left legacy of ten children of God." The Morris children and other relatives remained stoic through the services. The youngsters, still obviously shaken from the ordeal, steadfastly maintain that they will remain together. The story of the children's resolve to remain together is being told throughout the nation today with articles and pictures sent out by United Press International and requested individually by major newspapers in several cities. Response was scattered, but prompt from both residents of the community and strangers from other areas whose hearts go out to children. One man called immediately after hearing of the tragedy and offered his seven-bedroom home at Twain Harte to the family for as long as they could use it. A couple from Taft who have cared for foster children and now are alone in a large house, drove to Madera today to ask to be allowed to have the family live with them. Twenty-two dollars had arrived at the Bank of America by this morning for the trust fund established for the children; and Mrs. Fred Massetti, trustee for the fund, and friend of the family, said friends had pressed bills into her hand at the rosary Thursday night. The family has sought no money but established the trust fund in response to requests from friends that they be allowed to help in some way. Mrs. Massetti, emphasizing that no decisions have been made said this morning that she feels it would be marvelous if college educations for the older children, who will no doubt bare large part of the responsibility for their parent-less brothers and sisters, could be somehow assured. No decisions for the children's future are expected to be made until after summer school, which several of them are attending. Their paternal grandmother has arranged to stay with the children during this time. Family members have rallied to offer homes to the youngsters. They have already been offered homes in Concord, Fresno and New Jersey. Immediate relatives rushed to the house immediately to care for the children. The youngsters hope to somehow remain in Madera, their home for the past two years. Maderans, who have offered their help, hope too that they can.

10 Orphaned Children Don't Need Parents

WORLD'S SYMPATHY — The 10 Morris children look over a few of the hundreds of letters that poured in from all over the world after the death of their parents in a car accident.

Gus Zernial Here For Game

Big Gus Zernial and KPFK No Stars will make a special benefit appearance Saturday night for the Morris Family Trust Fund in a head-to-head softball duel with the Daily Tribune.

Nationwide Concern For Ten Children In Morris Family

Morris Fund Tops $20,000

$1,000!!
John Telzer of the Bank of America reaches around a mountain of contributions to the Morris Family Trust Fund.

Table At Bank Heaped With Morris Fund Letters

Anonymous $1,000 Donor To Trust Fund

Morris Fund At $36,700

Fund Reaches $3,000 For Orphaned Family

McClatchy Newspapers Service

MADERA — The special trust fund for the 16 orphaned children of Mr. and Mrs. Robert Morris, who were killed in an automobile accident in Fresno a week ago, has grown to more than $3,000 in a week, including a great number of $1 donations.

Mrs. Fred Maisetti, one of the administrators of the trust fund, said a number of offers to adopt the children have been received, including one from Washington, D.C.

She said, however, t h e children, ranging in age from 3 to 17, have said they desire to remain in Madera and have vowed to remain together.

The children, six girls and four boys, are being cared for by their paternal grandmother, Mrs. Mollie Morris, until more permanent arrangements can be made.

Donations to the trust fund are being received at t h e Madera Branch of the Bank of America.

Morris Family Trust Fund Passes $4,000 Total Mark

The Morris Family Trust fund has grown to approximately $4,000, according to John Tabor, an official of the Madera Bank of America. Today's mail had not yet open...

A two-inch stack of letter showed that donations are coming from Hawaii, Pennsylvania, Mississippi, New Hampshire, Nevada, Ohio, Pennsylvania, New Jersey, as well as throughout California. Tabor said...

Individual donations range from $1 to $250. Tabor has received two gifts of $250 one from Madera and the

other from the San Francisco area. The San Francisco bank official raising money for the fund has not yet sent in any...

$1,200 More For Fund

The Morris Family Trust fund increased another $1,200 today to a new total of $47,900

Recent contributions have included $700 from a Palo Alto A & W Root Beer stand which held a "Morris Family Fund Day" donating all proceeds, and $651 from the benefit barbecue sponsored by the Young Men's Institute.

Morris Case Familiar In All Parts Of Country

Proof of Madera's 16 orphans, the Morris children, has become so well known that a letter mailed in Brooklyn, N.Y. and addressed simply, "Many Morris, San Joaquin Valley," will arrive here safe and sound.

Proof of this was evidenced Monday when the local branch of the Bank of America received such a letter containing a contribution to the Morris Trust Fund which was sent to to aid the children after their parents were killed in a car crash near Fresno...

This and about 30 other contributions were received today at the bank bringing trust total up to $44,000...

A few more contributions were received today which have not yet been totaled, said the Bank of America handling the totals with Tabor in on vacation...

A final decision guardianship of the children is expected before the end month.

$34,150 For Morris Family, Car Wash Set

A surge in contributions to the Morris Family Trust Fund as the result of a nationwide television feature on the children was expected today.

Calls from New York, Tennessee, New Jersey and Florida were received this morning at the Bank of America in Madera where donations already had reached $1,500.

The 16 orphaned children of Robert and Joyce Morris were shown in a documentary aired on the CBS Walter Cronkite show Thursday night.

Morris Trust Fund At $39,500

The Morris Family Trust Fund climbed to $39,500 today, with sympathizers that it will top $40,000.

Another $600 amount raised at a barbecue by the Young Men's Institute has not yet been banked and added to the total.

Morris Children Trust Fund Is Now $45,900

John Tabor of the Bank of America reported today that the total...

Morris Trust Fund Total Now At $51,447

The Morris Family Trust Fund has reached a total $51,447 with thousands of individual persons and organizations, Bank of America officials say today. Total donations...

Cronkite Show Boosts Morris Fund

different types are slated for this weekend to help swell the fund, and the Young Men's Institute has sponsored a barbecue for July 20 when the clubs hope will raise another $500.

The Dominoes will play for a benefit dance tonight and two baseball games, the...

Morris Fund At $15,000

Contribution to the Morris Family Trust Fund were nearing the $15,000 mark this morning, Mrs. Fred Maisetti, a trustee, reported.

She said volunteers were still tabulating Monday's contributions and had a stack of mail which had arrived this morning to open yet.

The Gretsvrds dance band members Monday brought in $500 earned in benefit dance Friday night. Saturday night's benefit softball games netted $556.

Contributions are coming from throughout the nation, along with special offers such as a Palo Alto root beer stand owner's promise of our day's income. He is from a family of ten.

A citizen's band radio group in Fortuna, several of whose members also are busi...

Morris Fund At $44,500

Morris Funds

Mike and Pat Lindy held up the $48.20 given from a Jefferson Youth Club, sponsored for Fresno

worth. The funds will be turned over to the 16 children of Madera who were orphaned July 2 when their parents were killed in a traffic accident.
—Cody Tribune

★★★★ Army Boosts Returnee Early-Out to 5 Months

WASHINGTON (AP)—Many enlisted soldiers returning from South Vietnam will be discharged from service as much as five months earlier than their draft or enlistment tour calls for under an Army policy change announced Friday.

Present policy provides for early release of up to 90 days. The change goes into effect Aug. 1.

The early release regulation also applies to soldiers in South Korea and other "short tour" areas overseas. That's where a man serves less than 18 months if unaccompanied by his family or less than 24 months if he has his family with him. In Vietnam and Korea the duty tour is 12 months because of hazard and hardship.
(Continued on Back Page, Col. 3)

PACIFIC STARS AND STRIPES

AN AUTHORIZED PUBLICATION OF THE
U.S. ARMED FORCES IN THE FAR EAST

10¢

Vol. 24, No. 187   Sunday, July 7, 1968

Crowded Bridge Tumbles
200 SAVED IN LAKE

RESCUE WORKERS SEARCH WATERS OF LAKE SACAJEWEA FOR POSSIBLE VICTIMS AFTER FOOTBRIDGE COLLAPSED.

LONGVIEW, Wash. (AP)—A wooden footbridge jammed with people watching fireworks collapsed Thursday night, plunging scores of people into a lake near the center of Longview. All apparently survived.

Police Chief Ralph Benafiel said as many as 200 persons may have been on the bridge. But no one could know for certain.

Skindivers scoured Lake Sacajewea Friday but said they found no bodies. Ambulances, hearses and even station wagons were pressed into service, carrying 40 persons to Los Hospitals. Seven were admitted to St. John's Hospital for further treatment, two with broken legs.

The footbridge was 15 feet high, five feet wide and about 300 feet long. Water underneath was up to eight feet deep. There was no current.

The fireworks display, sponsored as in years past by the Jaycees, had just ended and Fourth of July celebrants were leaving the park that runs through the center of this pleasant, former company town when witnesses heard a loud snap.

The bridge bowed, sagged, and then went down. "There were a lot of screams. Mothers didn't know where their babies were. I heard people yelling, then it went down."

The footbridge was closed at week's end during recent years because of rotten timbers. Pieces of the bridge, nailed to shore Friday by a member, showed signs of rot.

(Continued on Back Page, Col. 3)

Blaiberg Has Lung Trouble

CAPETOWN, South Africa (AP) — The world's longest surviving heart transplant patient, Dr. Philip Blaiberg, 58, has developed lung complications.

A local hospital bulletin said early Saturday Dr. Blaiberg's liver condition is still improving, but he has developed pulmonary complications which are getting due to excess.

Blaiberg became the world's third heart transplant patient in jeopardy the hospital when he re...

Parents Killed in Smashup; 10 Orphans Stick Together

MADERA, Calif. (UPI)—"We want to stay together, father, don't let them separate us."

That, said the Rev. Salvatore Brusca on Thursday, was the tearful plea from the orphaned children of Mr. and Mrs. Robert G. Martin, 1940 Tuesday night in a headon crash.

Relatives, neighbors at St. Joachim's Catholic Church and

asked Junior, "That's who do all want to stay together."

While statements were being made for Friday's funeral the nuns indicated to try the children are not separated.

Everyone wants to keep those brothers and sisters one," said their aunt, Mrs. Tushovics in Fresno.

The children, who range in with Junior, Roberto, and grandmother.

Relatives added that the children, who remained in the family's white frame house just a block from the Madera Union High School last of the nine of 10 will be maintained. Since the accident, the relatives have said that they have lived with other relatives and neighbors ready to help.

A Short-Lived Demonstration

(text illegible)

Chapter 6

PEN PALS

The day the bank received a letter from Brooklyn, New York, addressed simply as "Kathy Morris, San Joaquin Valley," left no doubt that we put Madera on the map. We were famous for all the wrong reasons.

One afternoon we heard, "Knock, knock, may I come in?" through the screen door. An attractive woman in a navy-blue, A-line dress with white collar—clutching two paper bags in her right hand and a black patent leather handbag in the other—stood on the porch.

Grandma Morris, who was staying with us that week, and never one to hurry, sauntered to the door.

"Hello, were we expecting you?" Grandma asked in her low, raspy voice, worn rough from a lifetime of smoking.

"No, I'm sorry I didn't call ahead. My name is Mrs. Fonda. I'm from Bank of America. I brought something to share with the children."

Grandma let her in and called to those of us in the house—Judy, Linda, Mike, and me. It was a hot August afternoon. The rest of the kids were swimming at the high school, directly across the street.

"Would it be okay if we all sat at the dining room table?" Mrs. Fonda asked.

"Of course." Grandma motioned for us to sit.

"I've brought some letters from the people who donated to your trust fund. I thought you might like to read some of them and send thank you cards."

She placed one of the bags between Linda and me and a bag between Judy and Mike sitting across from us. Then she handed us pens and pads of paper. I picked up an envelope. A light blue map of Vietnam was on the left side. Red and blue stripes and United States Armed Forces Vietnam were imprinted across the bottom. Inside, pale blue stationery was watermarked with a map of Vietnam.

July 22, 1968

Dear Kathleen,

I read of your recent loss in the Stars & Stripes newspaper and would take this opportunity to extend my sincerest feelings to you and your family. A person can't realize what it is to lose someone until they have lost them.

If it is possible to keep the family together, that would be the thing to do. Were I in your place, that would be my feelings.

It is difficult to write, as I don't know you or your family. However, if there is any way at all that I might be of assistance to you, please let me know. I imagine you have gotten a lot of letters saying essentially the same thing, but, please consider mine, as I'd like to do something for your family. A little about myself: I'm 21, a GI in VietNam. My home is west Tennessee. If you need assistance in any way, just let me know.

I read the letter once, then twice. The guy was young and sounded so sincere. I'd never read anything so heartfelt before. I wondered what he looked like and why he wanted to help me. I honestly didn't know how to respond, so I picked up another letter. It was from a woman in North Dakota.

Dear Kathy and rest of the family,

We get the Bismarck tribune and I see this in the paper what happen to your parents. Has God forgotten orphan's? No God has not forgotten you. There is always somebody that's thinking of you. We are kinda interested of you children to give you a home. We live out in the country on a farm we raise wheat and corn and milk cows and do little of everything. Little information of us. We are in our 40's. We are a Catholic family. We belong to St. Peter Paul parish. We only have 1 boy Terry of our own he is 18 years old. And two little girls they are both adopted one is 9 years and one is 1 ½ years old. Children go to St Benedict school. We both grew up on a farm around here. My husband is Lawrence Welk's nephew. So

God bless you all. Kathy, if you find time drop me
a note to let me know if you have a home. I'll keep
you in my prayers.

Her words also tugged at my heartstrings and left me at a loss.
Flustered, I looked at Mrs. Fonda and asked, "What am I supposed to say?"

"Thank them for writing and their donation," she replied.

"But this guy in the Army wants to know if he can be of assistance. And this lady from North Dakota wants to adopt us. I don't
know what to say to them."

A pre-written thank you card that we simply signed would have
helped. We believed their heartfelt words deserved a proper and
lengthy response. So that's what we did—we wrote letters. To our cha-
grin, our letters prompted a lot of pen pals, especially with the soldiers.

With time I realized that for the letters to stop, I had to stop
responding. I felt guilty ignoring them, adding another pound to the
emotional baggage already packed with grief.

Chapter 7

MUTINY ON
THE BOUNTY

The fact that our parents left no money did not concern us. We lived our entire lives meagerly. The more significant issue was our parents did not have a will. No will meant we became wards of the court, under the auspices of the Department of Social Services. We were also assigned probation officers, just like juvenile delinquents who break the law. Our crime? Our parents died without a will.

On July 2, I went into shock and remained there for self-preservation. Thinking about my parents provoked unimaginable pain. Every morning was a haunting reminder that my parents were gone. Each day was like a spinning merry-go-round where my fingers gripped the metal bars while I hung on for dear life. Too painful to feel, I shut down and hid in a cocoon of impenetrable armor. Over time, I morphed from a free spirit living in a beautiful world to a phobic existing in a frightening world.

The ten of us were zombies going through the motions while we gripped a thin, fragile thread to reality. We worried that to cry or express our feelings would sever that connection. None of us understood we were already detached on a disconnected course.

It felt like nobody was interested in our emotional state. No adult hugged or cried with us. None of them talked about the accident. Nobody told us what to expect or how to deal with our grief. I understand now that my relatives were coping with their grief. But trained professionals, like social workers? Not one of them offered comfort or referred us to a counselor, psychologist, or someone to help us work through our pain.

Friends weren't there for us either. While attending summer school, my sisters said classmates stopped talking to them. Not knowing what to say, rather than try harder, they walked away.

The ten of us didn't fare much better as we weren't a touchy-feely family to begin with. We didn't hug, cry, or talk it out. I know I didn't cry because I distinctly remember thinking, *I'm so sad, but if I start crying, I'll never stop. I will cry for the rest of my life.*

⌁

We remained in our rented home in Madera for two months while the court grappled with our fate. Our grandmothers alternated living with us during that time. It was a tall order, caring for ten grandchildren while grieving the loss of their own children. It didn't help that the revolving door of reporters, social workers, and relatives made it feel more like Grand Central Station than a home.

An interesting dichotomy to our life in a fishbowl during those two months was that nobody watched us. All the activities made it a challenge for our grandmothers to keep tabs on the ten of us. Exhausted from the daily turmoil, they retired to bed early while we stayed up.

The chaos piled on top of grief created the perfect storm for our lives to implode. It didn't take long for the tight ship that our mother ran to turn into "mutiny on the bounty," with me leading the charge.

My siblings had always turned to me, so to look after them was second nature; however, the stream of people who relied on me for answers or interviews weighed me down and made each day more difficult to cope. Within a month, between my siblings and the adults, I was spread so thin that when my friends threw me a lifeline and invited me out, I jumped at the chance.

On the night they picked me up, the relentless thought of my parents being dead dissolved. I could breathe again. We rode around town with no destination and filled the car with teenage gossip, laughter, and cigarette smoke. As the hours grew long, I couldn't stomach the thought of going home and decided to stay out all night.

When my friends dropped me off at my house at sunrise, my "devil may care" attitude turned to terror. I feared I would get caught.

I turned the knob on the front door slow and steady, and leaned against it until a crack opened wide enough for me to peek inside. Nobody was up. I held my breath and tiptoed through the living room to my bedroom. Everyone was sound asleep. I crawled into bed, smug, triumphant, and gratified. My triumphant caper fueled my bravado to test the waters again the following week, when I smoked pot for the first time. My best friend and her boyfriend picked me up in his 1966 brown El Camino. We drove east on Highway 145 toward Millerton

Lake, where there was nothing but twenty miles of flatland on either side of the road. A two-lane stretch perfect for drag races or, in our case, getting high.

When I had parents, sneaking out of the house or staying out all night didn't occur to me. Sex, drugs, and alcohol crossed my mind, but I was too chicken to experiment. Surely, I would get caught or pregnant. My parents had been my moral compass. I did not want to hurt them or get punished. The disappointment on their faces or the thought of getting grounded kept me on the straight and narrow. With them gone, I felt I didn't have anyone to be good for. I believed I was free to do whatever I wanted. Soon, my siblings followed suit.

One of my sisters ran away. She did not have a good relationship with our grandparents to begin with. She believed Grandma Lachawicz hated her because she always picked on her over trivial things like my sister ordering a hamburger rather than trying something new. Moreover, she detested that Grandma belittled our dad and asked meddling questions. After the accident, when Grandma told adults she had a great relationship with our father, my sister wrote "hypocrite" on a piece of paper and taped it to the refrigerator. When our grandmother found it, she ripped it from the fridge and stormed into the living room to show our grandfather. Grandpa, his face beet red, wagged his finger inches from my sister's nose, and scowled, "Look at the devil in your eyes! Judas! That's who you are!"

Terrified, my sister ran three miles to a friend's house and stayed for a week. Surprisingly, or perhaps tellingly, my grandparents did not force her to return.

While we kids acted out, tension began to brew among the relatives. Opposite sides of the family pulled us aside to ask who we wanted to live with. When they discovered that they were all doing the same thing, they stopped talking to each other. The friction between the adults added more strain on us kids.

In early August, Grandpa and Grandma Lachawicz filed a petition for custody. We knew them best because we spent our entire lives around them—holidays, vacations, and birthdays. For them to file was not a surprise, but it was confusing. I didn't understand where they planned on putting ten kids in their two-bedroom, one-bath, one thousand square foot house. Aunt Mary was in high school and still lived at home. Perhaps they thought someone would give them a bigger house because many strangers offered theirs or offered to build one. A more plausible explanation was they had a plan.

If granted custody, they planned to divide us. Some with our grandparents and the remainder with Uncle Steve in New Jersey and Uncle Gene in Fresno.

My sister overheard our grandparents and uncles discussing their plan to divide us and told Aunt Glo, Dad's oldest sister. In response, Aunt Glo and Uncle Stan filed a petition for custody. Both in their forties, they were easygoing and hip. Their home in the Bay Area was twice the size of our grandparents and had a built-in pool.

While the chasm deepened between both sides of the family, gifts began to accumulate for us, or, as the adults called them—bribes. Uncle Steve, our mother's brother, a buyer with Kinney Shoes, sent giant cardboard boxes filled with shoes. White Keds, Buster browns, and black patent leather for the girls. Wingtips and Joe Lapchick sneakers for the boys.

Our grandparents took us to Disneyland, courtesy of their life insurance group. The Disney characters greeted us for photo ops at the entrance. We were treated like royalty at the Disneyland Hotel and had separate rooms with an open tab for room service.

Aunt Glo brought toys and games such as Pick Up Sticks, Operation, and Etch A Sketch. Chatty Cathy dolls and jacks for the girls. Corn cob pipes, matchbox cars, and G.I. Joe soldiers for the boys. However, the best gift she gave us was the weekend in the California Delta on her houseboat.

Our aunt and uncle owned a forty-foot blue and white pontoon houseboat. It was a boxy rectangular shape with a patio in front and a sunbathing deck on top. Inside was a set of bunk beds, kitchen, bathroom, and a dining table that converted to a bed. None of us had ever been on a boat so their announcement to take us out for the weekend was exhilarating.

The day we left our suffocating, stifling house of despair for the crisp air and rolling green terrain of northern California was nothing short of spectacular. We ran like escaped caged animals when we arrived at the Martinez Marina. The wooden dock swayed over the water as we skipped to the boat, all of us happy as pigs in a new mudhole.

Once we loaded the groceries and sleeping bags onto the boat, Uncle Stan took his place behind the wheel and shouted orders. "All hands on deck! Robert and Mike, untie the ropes from the dock!"

"Aye aye, Captain!" Mike replied in his best Popeye, the Sailor Man voice.

The boys knelt and untied the white nylon ropes.

"Now, jump back into the boat and pull in the bumpers!" The boys followed his commands like seasoned seadogs—their chests puffed with pride.

The boat pulled away from its berth and transported us to pages straight out of *Huckleberry Finn*. Everywhere we looked was a feast for the eyes. Cottonwood, sycamore, and blackberry vines lined the riverbanks. Hawks, blackbirds, and geese soared overhead. Flocks of cranes stood ankle-deep in the murky green water.

An hour later, our uncle dropped anchor at his favorite fishing spot on the Sacramento River. "Grab a fishing pole, boys!" The universe must have known the boys were starving for joy because they hit pay dirt! Every time my brothers cast, they caught a fish. Their cheers and laughter echoed off the water while the ice chest filled with a bounty of bass, trout, and catfish.

At sundown, Uncle Stan found a spot for the night, tied off the boat, and lowered a cage baited with hot dogs into the water. The next day he was rewarded with a basket of olive-brown lobster-like creatures called crawdads. While the boys poked them with sticks, our aunt placed a big aluminum stock pot filled with water on the stove and turned it on.

"Boys! Bring me the cage!" Uncle Stan yelled a half-hour later. Steam rose in the galley from the boiling water. He reached into the basket, picked up a crawdad wildly brandishing its claws, and dropped it into the pot.

"What are you doing?" we girls screamed in disbelief. "They're still alive!"

"That's the way you cook 'em," Uncle Stan said calmly.

"Can they feel that? Are they screaming?" Tenderhearted Theresa could barely watch.

"No, they're fine. They die instantly," he chuckled.

"Look! They're turning red!" Squealed Roberta and covered her mouth with her hand.

After the crawdads were cooked, our aunt spread them out on a newspaper placed on the dining table. Uncle Stan demonstrated how to twist the tail, remove the white meat, and dip them in clarified butter. We followed his instructions, popped the morsels into our mouths, and discovered the most delicious and delectable food of our lives. Sweet, tasty, and mild. The new cuisine, like the boat trip, was another adventure to be savored.

After sundown, we snuggled in our sleeping bags and spun tales of flying saucers into the wee hours of the night. After everyone drifted to sleep, I lay alone, wishing the night would never end. The royal black night was like oil paint thickly layered on canvas. Bright twinkling stars cast their magic through pinholes upstaged only by shooting stars that left trails of light etched across the night sky. Cottonwood leaves rustled in the breeze while a symphony of groaning bullfrogs blended with cricket chirps. Encapsulating all was the distinct marshy smell of the river. Not especially pleasurable, but grounding in good ways—earthy, water-born, and rough-hewn. Distinctly different. And different was a welcome repose.

Chapter 8

THE DECISION

While we stole moments of happiness on the Delta, Grandma Lachawicz was busy degrading us to social workers. When questioned about our character and personality, she gave her suspicions or opinions, rather than facts. She said one of my sisters was a lesbian because of her close bond with a friend and described the sister who ran away as stubborn, obstinate, and selfish.

When we returned from our weekend away with our aunt and uncle, the social workers conveyed the information gleaned from our grandmother. Enraged, my sisters made it clear they did not want to live with our grandparents. And none of us wanted to deal with Aunt Mary, Mom's sister. She was eighteen years younger than our mother and raised as an only child. An indulged teenager did not mesh well with our team of ten—especially with us older girls.

Six weeks after the accident, a social worker and probation officer arrived at our home with marching orders. Their job was to provide a recommendation to the judge on where to place us. They had much to consider—information gathered from Grandma, custody petitions from our grandparents and aunt, and hundreds of offers to adopt or foster us. I imagine they felt tremendous pressure knowing they were under the microscope as thousands of people had invested in our fate.

The social worker, a tall, heavy-set woman with a beehive hairstyle and cat-rimmed glasses, wore a drab brown dress that hit below her knees. The probation officer, a thin man in disheveled white shirt and grey slacks, accompanied her. They instructed the adults to leave and gathered the ten of us in the living room.

The woman spoke first. "My name is Mrs. Neal, and this is Mr. Schafer. It is our job to tell the judge where to place you. Your grandparents and your Aunt Glo have both asked that you live with them. We will give you a piece of paper and a pen. I want you to write the name of the person you want to live with—your aunt or your grandparents. Do not show your brothers and sisters what you have written. Hold up your paper when you're done, and we will collect it from you."

They passed out paper and pens and repeated the instructions. Eddie, three years old, had no say. The rest of us were old enough to understand and write. We wrote down our preferences, held up our paper, and watched as they collected them. Once they had them all, they turned their backs to us and tallied the votes. The exercise was a waste of time because we knew we were not in agreement before their poll.

Mrs. Neal turned around, studied us, and took a deep breath. "It looks like you kids are divided."

Linda, not one to hold back, spoke first. "We knew that. We talked about it."

"Is that what you want? To get split up? Some of you living with your grandparents and the rest living with your aunt?" she asked.

Our response was quick and loud, "No!"

"The other kids just need to change their minds," I said. "Most of us want to live with Aunt Glo." I kissed Eddie's forehead, then shifted his body on my lap while he raised his eyes to meet mine. "Everything's okay, Eddie," I assured him.

"Why don't you want to live with your grandparents?" asked Mr. Schafer.

Judy jumped up and used both hands to straighten her plaid yellow pedal pushers. "Because Mary is a spoiled brat! No way am I living with her!" She plopped down in the chair with her nose in the air.

Mrs. Neal raised her eyebrows. Mr. Schafer cleared his throat.

Together they turned to address the little kids sitting cross-legged and barefoot on the carpet. "Why don't you want to live with your Aunt Glo?"

"Because I want to live with Grandma," Eight-year-old Jeff pouted and crossed his arms.

"If you can't agree on which relative you want to live with, we have plenty of offers from others who want you to live with them. Some people in Madera have offered to take you in. Is that something you would like?" asked Mr. Schafer. He glanced down at the papers in his hands as if reading the names.

"No!" I was quick to respond. "I hate Madera. I haven't liked it since we moved here. I liked San Jose a lot better."

"Okay, people have offered to build houses. Kathi, you could be the nanny. How do you feel about that?" Mrs. Neal asked as she looked over the top of her glasses.

What? Are you kidding me? I have been counting the days till I turn eighteen. Eddie is three. A fifteen-year life sentence? Am I supposed to do that? When is it my turn to have fun? Filled instantly with guilt, I thought for a moment before responding.

"No! I'm tired of being a mother! I don't think that's a good idea at all!" My tone made it clear it would never be an option.

"There are plenty of families across the country who have offered to foster or adopt all of you. Would you like that?" she countered.

"No!" several of us said in unison.

"Why does that not interest you?"

"Because we don't know them," Theresa replied, then scooted closer to Carole, who sat beside her on the sofa.

"What about splitting you up? You older girls move to New Jersey with your Uncle Steve, and the younger ones live with Uncle Gene." Mrs. Neal shoved her hand in her pocket and tapped one foot.

We all responded, "No!"

"Why not?"

I blew out an exasperated sigh and said, "Because we wouldn't be happy!"

Mrs. Neal stiffened, widened her stance, put both hands on her hips and snarled through clenched teeth, "Who said children should be happy?"

My mouth dropped to the floor. *Did I hear you right? Did you just ask "Who said children should be happy?" to ten kids who just lost their mother and father? What kind of social worker are you?*

None of us had ever been in trouble. After school, church, and Catechism, we did our homework and chores. Our parents had instilled that we respect and obey adults. I kept my mouth shut while my head spun with the realization that our fate could be in the hands of a cold, callous bitch.

The following week, Judge Hammerberg escorted us into the courtroom and questioned us again. We were armed and ready. Those of us who wanted to live with Aunt Glo had campaigned for everyone to vote for our aunt. It didn't take a lot of convincing. After the encounter with the social worker, we understood that if we didn't vote alike, the judge might separate us.

Judge Hammerberg awarded us to Aunt Glo on August 28, 1968. We waited two months for that decision.

It took five months to unravel.

Chapter 9

LEAVING THE
PAST BEHIND

The judge stated that he based his decision on the probation department's recommendation. He added that he did not award us to our grandparents because of their age. They were both sixty-one, so he feared that three-year-old Eddie might spend his teenage years with substitute parents.

The judge granted Aunt Glo custody because he believed a relative, rather than a stranger, would provide the "love, affection, and guidance" of persons of our own blood. Aunt Glo, a tall, proud, and attractive redhead, our blood relative, may as well have been an alien. She and Uncle Stan were strangers as much as anyone else who asked to foster or adopt us. I saw them more in the two months after the accident than I had in my entire seventeen years. Right or wrong, I was happy Aunt Glo won custody and relieved that we could move on with our lives.

After listening to the judge's decision, we marched out of the courtroom into a sea of reporters. Television and newspaper correspondents from United Press International, Associated Press, CBS, and NBC were waiting with cameras and microphones. Exhausted from weeks of publicity, I deflected all the attention with detached fatigue. *I don't want to do this anymore* dominated my thoughts as I made my way outside.

Nobody forewarned me that Terry Drinkwater, a CBS news correspondent, requested an interview. Or if they did, I didn't care. My eyes were dead batteries, too drained to see beyond my disjointed footsteps. Had I understood the interview would be shown nationwide on *CBS Evening News with Walter Cronkite*, I might have faked enthusiasm.

Once we took our positions on the lawn outside the courthouse, Drinkwater asked me, "What do you think life will be like for all ten of you up there?"

"It will go on the same. I don't think it will really change. I don't know," I replied through narrowed eyes. The afternoon sun blinded me when I looked up at him.

"Are you happy?"

"Yeah, I am," I lied while my mind screamed, *please go away and leave me alone.*

The entire court system was foreign to me, to all of us. Although we were awarded to our aunt, legal custody and guardianship remained with the probation and welfare departments. Most unsettling was that we were assigned Probation Officers. The trust fund, with contributions from as far away as South Vietnam and West Germany, grew little after that day. As with most fifteen minutes of fame, we were over and old news in the public's consciousness.

After court, we returned home and packed our clothes, beds, and dressers for our move to Concord. I was numb, merely going through the motions, so when Aunt Glo asked if I wanted to take anything else, I couldn't think of a thing.

It is a sad fact that, as a displaced orphan, I didn't have the energy, experience, or insight to know what tools I might need to forge ahead. I didn't understand that in the years to follow, my parents' personal belongings, which held their scent, might ease my grief. Or objects that held their spirit might shepherd me through my darkest hours. I didn't have the foresight to know that my dad's die-cast model cars, a book with my mother's writing, or a table my parents built might be invaluable keepsakes for my siblings and me.

My mother had beautiful penmanship. I was as much intrigued by the artistic flow of her pen as I was with what she wrote. One day, while she and I sat at the dinner table, I asked, "Mom, how did you get such beautiful handwriting?"

"When I went to St. Clare's School in Chicago, we had to practice hundreds of hours, tracing over letters until we could write them perfectly," she replied. Then she turned her face upward, as if to contemplate an exhaustive discipline from a time long ago.

"We had to practice too, Mom, but my handwriting does not look like yours."

In Madera, the den had shelves spanning the length of the wall crammed with books. Bored one summer, I looked for something to read and spotted an unfamiliar green hardback. I pulled it out and thumbed through it. Writing (unquestionably my mother's) laced the white spaces. Shocked—to write in a book was a cardinal sin—I rushed to show her.

She was in the dining room, starching and ironing Dad's white dress shirts. I laid the book on the ironing board, opened it to a page, and pointed. "Mom! Isn't this your handwriting?"

"Yes, it is," she replied.

"Why did you write in this book? We would get in trouble for that!"

"When our family moved from Chicago to California, I took books to read. I wanted to remember everything as we traveled, so I wrote in that book wherever I could find space."

Inscribed between paragraphs and around the edges of the pages was a journal. It wasn't a neat and organized record, but a documentary just the same, written when Mom was fourteen years old. She recorded her thoughts and the places they visited during their ten-day journey—an insightful pathway to the essence of my mother. I'm sad that I cannot recall one detail and that none of my siblings ever saw that book.

Another keepsake was a coffee table that my parents built together. They created a mosaic for the top of a circular wooden table with three legs. Every evening, they sat side by side on the sofa, hunched over a pile of blue tiles, and used tile cutters to break them into smaller bits. They pieced the tile together like a jigsaw puzzle and celebrated when the fragments fit perfectly. I remember them locking eyes and beaming with pride as the mosaic progressed and hugging when it was complete. Like a prized trophy, their masterpiece sat proudly in the center of the living room.

The journal and coffee table were left behind. So were my dad's diecast model cars—his only hobby besides fishing. When we moved, everything was left in the house for others to take. Articles that held my parents' memory or fingerprints were given or thrown away. Of no value to anyone else but priceless to us, those precious articles could have helped with our healing.

There were no family meetings to discuss how to divide items of obvious value. It was more of a first-come, first-serve basis. Although some of my siblings acquired a few things—like our parent's wedding rings and some clothes—the little kids walked away with nothing.

Relatives took our heirlooms like the family bible, boxes of photographs, and the statue of the Blessed Mother that Judy clung to the night of the accident. In later years, when we asked them to return what was rightfully ours, they denied possession, even though we had seen the items in their home.

Some keepsakes eventually found their way back to us, usually when relatives died. But by then, we were jaded and covered with battle scars. We needed the mementos when our wounds were fresh.

Grandma Morris received the flag that covered our father's coffin. Nobody told us that she died five years after our parents, and no one returned the flag. It's gone forever.

It may as well have been a tornado that hit our home on July 2. We lost everything. Not one adult had the foresight to ensure that all ten of us came away with something, anything, belonging to our parents. The ten of us left Madera and all evidence of our parents behind.

Chapter 10

SHE DIDN'T FOLLOW THE RULES

The court order granting our aunt custody of us included three directives. She did not honor any of them.

The first directive was that Grandma Morris was to move out of Aunt Glo's house. Grandma did not leave. She was sixty-one-years-old, the housekeeper and cook. She did not have a driver's license or own a car. Her only income was a small monthly Social Security check.

The rationale behind the directive made sense. It was to make room for the ten of us in our aunt's four-bedroom house. However, it felt cruel to order Grandma out of the home she had lived in for years. Aunt Glo had no intention of asking her mother to leave. We didn't want her to go either. Kind, soft-spoken, and reticent, she embodied all things good. Her gentle temperament was a calm salve at a time when our lives were in turmoil.

The second directive was to uphold our Catholic faith. We were expected to attend Catechism on Saturday mornings and Mass on Sundays as we had done our entire lives. Aunt Glo had no religious affiliation and did not frequent any place of worship. She asked us once if we wanted to go to Catechism and church. Of course, we said no, and she was happy to oblige. What child, after getting up early for school all week long, doesn't look forward to sleeping in and playing on the weekends? What kid would willingly trade Saturday morning cartoons like Bugs Bunny, Scooby-Doo, and The Flintstones for Catechism? Especially at Aunt Glo's.

All our lives, we spent Saturday mornings studying religion. When we returned home, we were not allowed to play until we finished our chores. At Aunt Glo's, Grandma was the housekeeper! Our weekends, for the first time in our lives, were days of leisure.

The third directive was to attend Catholic schools. Aunt Glo enrolled us in public schools. I'm not sure why, but it was fine by me. In my twelve years of schooling, I attended a private school for only one—eighth grade at Saint John's Catholic school in Fresno, the year I spent paralyzed in fear.

I loved school. What I didn't love was attention or risking embarrassment. Shy does not adequately describe my childhood and adolescent self. In kindergarten, I did not participate in show-and-tell because I was terrified to stand in front of the class, let alone talk. The embarrassment of giving the wrong answer was crushing. When a teacher asked the class a question, I tried to shrink by sliding as far under the desk as possible. With lowered head and downcast eyes, I covered my face with my hair, hand, or jacket—anything to hide. My heart beat double time as my mind begged *please don't call on me!* The tactics worked most of the time, and most of the time, I enjoyed school. Going to school meant getting out of the house, not doing chores, or watching kids.

My eighth-grade year at Saint John's had been like jumping down a rabbit hole. Nothing at that private school resembled anything I had ever known. We wore uniforms—white shirts and navy-blue skirts and jackets. We stood at attention when a nun or priest walked into the room. You could hear a pin drop once the class was in session.

The nuns wore stiff habits, stern faces, and carried a ruler—habits like those in the movie *The Sound of Music*. Layers of black fabric skimmed the ground topped with white bibs. No skin was visible except for their faces and hands. I studied their heads, searching for a wisp of hair, trying to escape from under the wide band that surrounded their faces. After a year of close examination with no evidence, I decided they must be bald, making them more mysterious and sinister.

My teacher, Sister Marian, towered over me. Heavyset and substantial, her presence and no-nonsense attitude frightened me. A large crucifix hung around her neck and a long rosary from her waist. Not the pretty sparkling rosaries that we clamored for with pink or purple glass beads and five decades that fit in the palm of your hand. Hers was made of large wooden beads, fifteen decades and four feet long when laid out. They rattled when she walked, like the keys of a prison guard. And walk she did—up and down the aisles of our neatly arranged desks. Checking our work and calling on us from behind. With her behind me, my tried-and-true tactics for hiding were of no use. I spent eighth grade mortified and jumped out of my seat each time her ruler smacked a desk. I vowed I would never again attend a Catholic school.

To continue in public schools was perfectly fine by me!

Chapter 11

AUNT GLO'S

Although only one hundred seventy-five miles separate Madera from Concord, they are as different as the fires of Purgatory and the third level of Paradise. Madera, the center of California in the San Joaquin Valley, is rural, hot, and flat with an economy based primarily on agriculture. Concord, surrounded by lush natural beauty, is a dynamic suburb of San Francisco with a pleasant Mediterranean climate. Industry driven, it is progressive and sophisticated in comparison.

I considered myself a big city girl. Dad, a manager for rapidly expanding Kinney Shoes, transferred every six months for their grand openings. In the 1950s, we lived in southern California. We moved to cities within greater Los Angeles: Anaheim, Garden Grove, and Inglewood, to name a few. When I turned nine in 1960, Dad transferred to northern California: Stockton, Vallejo, and San Jose. By then, I was comfortable living in sprawling cities, swallowed up and detached from everyone. In 1965, before my freshman year in high school, we moved to Madera. Boring and small with fifteen thousand nosey residents, it was not a good fit for me. I hated living there from day one.

All ties with Madera severed the day my parents were killed. Left with few friends, exhausted from the revolving door of reporters, social workers, and bickering relatives, I wanted to run away from everything and everybody. I felt like I was suffocating. Much like a day when I was twelve years old, and the neighborhood bully held me underwater. I doubt that I was indeed on the brink of death, but while restrained underwater, I believed otherwise. My sisters peeled his hands from my thrashing body, and with his grip released, I surfaced, gasping for air. After the accident, Madera, always despised, aligned with that day.

Festering beneath it all was pent-up restlessness. Counting down my eighteenth birthday began my first year of high school. Sentenced to a life of servitude with cooking, cleaning, and watching kids, I longed to escape and experience adventure like Thor, in my favorite book *Kon-Tiki*.

My yearning deepened following my parents' death. I longed to leave the black abyss of Madera where I would surely suffocate and die.

⌣

We left Madera for Aunt Glo's one week before school started. Anxious to leave the past behind and curious as to what lay ahead, all of us crammed into our aunt's orange and white Volkswagen bus. We traveled from the dried yellow flatlands to the vibrant green undulating hills of the Bay Area on Highway 580 where two lanes became eight, and people sped through the turns like slot cars.

Our aunt and uncle's induction into their new life was the three-hour trip surrounded by an energetic mob. Ten kids uprooted from a quiet town to the urban hustle and bustle—their life, upended with the hustle and bustle of ten kids.

Two and a half hours into the ride, Eddie asked, "How much longer, Auntie Glo?"

"We're almost there, honey. Another half-hour, and we'll be home."

We're almost home. Home. I placed my hand between the glass and the window frame and pushed the window open. The bus filled with cool air. *Will living with Aunt Glo ever feel like home?*

We exited the freeway early afternoon and made our way through tidy streets lined with shade trees. When we parked in the driveway of their prim two-story house, I knew I wasn't in Kansas anymore.

⌣

Growing up, I didn't realize we were poor. I did not feel deprived or think I was below anyone else. I attribute my sense of equality to my parents—especially my mom. She went without to ensure we dressed well. She gifted us with clothes for our birthdays, not toys. For Easter, she bought us dress shoes, gloves, and hats. The outfits were perfect for Mass and special occasions. For Christmas, she bought us pajamas and slippers. Dad managed shoe stores, so we always had good shoes.

We didn't eat steak, but we never went hungry. We couldn't afford expensive vacations, so we frequented parks, the beach, and drive-in movies where a station wagon stuffed with a ton of lively kids cost a buck to get in.

Mom stuffed brown paper bags with freshly made popcorn smothered in melted butter. There was no such thing as premade bagged popcorn back then. We brought treats enjoyed on rare occasions—five-cent candy bars like Big Hunks and Abba-Zaba. Our communal drink was from Dad's steel thermos. Filled with cherry Kool-Aid, we poured it into the black lid and passed it around.

We kids dressed in our pajamas, folded down the seats in the station wagon, and piled onto a sea of pillows and blankets. At the drive-in, Dad drove the aisles until he found a spot with a perfect view of the screen. He reached outside, grabbed the small silver speaker that hung on a stand between cars, placed it on top of the glass, rolled the window up, and adjusted the volume.

While we nestled in for two features, the little kids, tucked snugly between warm bodies and blankets, were lucky to last through the first. At intermission, we played on the swings under the big screen or hurried to the snack bar to use the restroom. Our excursion to the movies was as memorable as a day in Disneyland.

Our struggle with money was evident in where and how we lived. Decent single-story rentals in acceptable neighborhoods most of the time. Piss poor rentals in borderline neighborhoods at other times. Mismatched and worn furniture. Twin beds that we shared. One dresser per bedroom with each of us assigned one drawer. Pull-down shades or thin curtains covered the windows. School artwork or family photographs decorated the walls.

We had an above-ground pool in San Jose. Before that, roasting pans served as swimming pools. When we moved to Stockton, our parents bought their first house in a neighborhood with a community pool. It was short-lived. Dad was transferred a year later to Vallejo.

The house in Stockton, the only home we owned and the nicest home we lived in, did not compare to Aunt Glo's.

⤳

Our aunt and uncle's neighborhood left no doubt that we had been transported to a new world. Everywhere I looked were green manicured lawns, rose bushes, and expensive cars sitting in the driveways. Every home was larger and nicer than anything we ever lived in or visited. Aunt Glo's stately house had a façade of red brick and red double doors. White pillars standing tall and proud like a couple of queen's guards supported the covered porch's weight.

Inside our cousin Brad, their fifteen-year-old son, and Grandma Morris waited for our arrival. When they opened the door, it revealed a staircase and a living room to the right. Kids dashed through the opening. The younger ones sprinted upstairs to check out the three bedrooms and bathroom while the rest of us explored the first floor.

Their backyard had a built-in rectangular pool with a diving board and a deck surrounding it. The only greenspace was a three-foot raised flowerbed with roses and strawberries running the length of the back fence.

As soon as the kids spotted the clear blue water reflecting the afternoon sun, they pushed open the patio door and ran outside. Carole, the tomboy, put one knee on the deck and shoved her hand in the water.

"Perfect!" Then she stood up, shook her hand, and sprayed water all over Linda's starched shirt. Linda's eyes opened wide, and then her mouth.

"You punk! I'm going to get you!" Linda fisted her hand then pounced.

Carole took off running with Linda hot on her heels. Carole was the fastest runner of us all. Nobody could catch her.

"Can we go swimming?" Mike pleaded.

"Yeah, can we please?" Jeff chimed in.

"Not today," Uncle Stan answered. "The movers will be driving up any minute. Everyone needs to unpack!"

Roberta swayed gently with Eddie on the lounge swing at the far end of the patio. They looked content under the shaded pergola. Eleven-year-old Roberta had long ago taken Eddie under her wing.

In sharp contrast to our thrift store furniture, our aunt and uncle's furniture was chic and cosmopolitan. The family room had an orange leather sofa, yellow chairs, and a color console television. Built-in bookshelves painted orange graced both sides of the red brick fireplace.

In the living room, a foot-long iridescent Arowana glided gracefully through the water in a fish tank built into the wall. Heavy tan drapes woven with gold filigree and a valance with gold tassels covered the expansive window.

Each bedroom had matching ensembles in either maple or white wicker. Hanging above the landing in the stairwell was a large, round multi-colored Chinese paper lantern.

Photographs by Brad and our uncle hung on the walls. Not the typical studio-type shots, but thought-provoking art, like a girl's silhouette, bright pink, arms outstretched toward the sky against a black backdrop. Another picture was a headshot of Brad's sister, our cousin Lucy, at the 1967 Monterey Pop Festival. She stared pensively into the camera with her face painted white with red, yellow, and black patterns around her eyes, mouth, and cheeks. Flowers in her hair. Intrigued by her appearance and gaze, I tried to imagine what she was like. Later that day, my curiosity was rewarded.

Lucy zipped into the driveway in her white convertible. She bounced out of the sports car dressed in full psychedelic regalia. Barefoot and wearing no makeup, Lucy wore flowered bell-bottoms and countless beaded bracelets. She jingled as she pranced around, personifying everything I'd heard about hippies. This colorful and animated creature put the exclamation point on our transport to another planet.

The entire house, furnishings, and Lucy's garb were unlike anything I had ever seen. We were like foreign exchange students experiencing a different culture. It felt that different.

When the moving van arrived, everyone sprang into action. On the spot decisions were made as we unloaded the truck. Theresa and Roberta agreed to share a blue sofa bed in the den. The four oldest girls—Judy, Linda, Carole, and I—divvied up the largest bedroom. I liked its quirky triangular-shaped ceiling. Teenage Brad grudgingly moved into a bedroom with my young brothers Robert, Mike, and Jeff. Three-year-old Eddie and Grandma shared the smallest bedroom.

The following week, everyone returned to their regular routines. We started school. Our aunt returned to her job with Bazar, a discount department store. Our uncle returned to his position with Moore Business Forms in Emeryville, a half-hour away.

It was Grandma's life that changed the most. Before we moved in, she earned her keep by maintaining the house for four. With our invasion, her load increased to fourteen. Added to her responsibilities was caring for three-year-old Eddie.

I didn't consider how taxing it must have been on her. I was too busy celebrating! The chains were broken! All jobs previously held by me were relinquished to her. For the first time in my life, I didn't return home after school to a list of chores, kids to watch, or meals to prepare. My life shifted in a monumental way when we moved to Concord.

While everyone struggled to find a rhythm and their niche in our newly formed family, personalities, attitudes, and conflicts began to emerge. It's difficult to adjust in any circumstance when people share the same space. On short notice, it proved to be impossible with ten orphans, an unhappy teenager, indifferent foster parents, and an overworked grandmother in the mix.

Uncle Stan, a tall, intelligent, and quiet man, hid in the shadows of Aunt Glo. Handsome with light brown wavy hair and green eyes, he smoked and kept to himself. He played the trumpet, made sourdough bread, and ate a bowl of cereal every night before going to bed. A machinist during the week, he kept a low profile on the weekends.

On our one family outing, an overnight camping trip at Half Moon Bay, he surprised us at sunset. He stood on the crest of a dune with his trumpet held high and played taps. Crisp notes pierced the ocean air. His silhouette against the kaleidoscopic sky awash with flamingo pink and crimson orange remains etched in my mind.

Although a pleasant man, he was aloof and distant. Not once did he take us on their houseboat as he had during the custody battle. His lack of interaction, especially with the boys, led me to believe that fostering us was not his decision and that maybe our trip to the Delta had been a bribe.

Aunt Glo, a tall, attractive, fiery redhead, worked all week as an office manager and returned home to dinner, a clean house, and no laundry, courtesy of Grandma. Her single household job was to cook dinner on the weekends. Self-assured, she had a presence about her that commanded attention. Intimidating, anyone who crossed her was met with controlled rage and icy silence. You could count on her holding a grudge indefinitely.

Our aunt was not as distant as our uncle, but her working outside of the home left little time to interact with us kids. They took us to

Shakey's Pizza a couple of times, but other than that, I cannot recall them spending quality time with us.

Brad was not a fan of us moving in. He was a sophomore in high school and accustomed to his life as an only child after his older sister married. He was vocal about his contempt for sharing his bedroom with our three young brothers and avoided us most of the time.

Grandma, widowed thirty years earlier, never remarried or worked. She had five children. Aunt Glo was the oldest, and Dad was the middle child. She was slim, 5'7", and had short dark hair. A chain smoker, she had a bad habit of lighting a cigarette, taking a few puffs, then leaving it in the ashtray to burn up. Grandma had a deeply creased face, a raspy voice, and no teeth. She didn't wear dentures, and oddly enough, none of us thought that was strange. As a young woman, she lost the tip of her middle finger, the entire first knuckle, in a meat grinder. We thought it was the coolest thing ever and begged her to show us at every opportunity.

Grandma liked to play the slot machines at Harrah's in Reno. She rode a chartered bus and brought back stacks of silver dollars. Her weekly outing was to play Bingo every Friday night at the American Legion Hall. Often, she asked me to drive her and sometimes asked me to stay. I enjoyed my time with her and the silver dollars she paid me for gas.

As Grandma moved throughout the house, she often grumbled under her breath about how tired she was. Who could blame her? While the rest of us were at school or work, she was home all day caring for a toddler while she cleaned and did the laundry. She was expected to have dinner ready when our aunt and uncle got home from work. When we got home from school, she had little time and no energy to interact with us. Although she was a pleasant woman, she rarely spoke as she went about her business and retired to her room early.

In a new world where adults faded into the woodwork, I was free to play.

Chapter 12

EVOLUTION

We moved to Concord in time for me to begin my senior year in high school. By that time, I had gone to nine different schools and was used to being the new girl, whether I liked it or not. To leave Madera, where I had few friends, was not upsetting.

The office of Pleasant Hill High School is where I encountered my first fan. While I stood in line to enroll, a boy standing a few feet away stared at me. I caught him studying me several times before he approached and exclaimed, "I know you! I saw you on TV! You're one of the ten Morris orphans, aren't you?" I was taken aback and intrigued at the same time. *Wow! I'm two hundred miles from Madera, and this guy knows who I am.*

For seven years, people either recognized me from television or by my name. Countless times I was asked if I was one of the ten Morris orphans. It was always a rollercoaster of emotions when it happened. Although flattered that I was recognized, I was also saddened by the reminder that my parents were dead. After all, that was the only reason they knew who I was.

ᘯ

A month after we moved to Concord, Aunt Sandy, Aunt Glo's sister, gave me my first car. We named it "the blue bomb" because it was mechanically challenged and had a hood that extended into tomorrow. It might have been a 1960 Ford Fairlane. I don't recall the type of car as much as I remember the good times I had with my sisters, especially our trips to and from Pleasant Hill High school.

"Hey, Kathi! How much gas do we have?" Judy asked while opening the car door.

"You know damn good and well that I have no clue, Judy Denise!" The broken gas gauge and dying starter meant driving on a hope and a prayer.

"Well, I'm not going to help push this piece of junk if we run out of gas again!"

"Then get out! This is a family affair!" I lit a cigarette while she and my sisters argued over who was riding shotgun.

"Do you have to smoke? It smells up my hair and clothes!" Judy's complaining was never-ending.

"Smoke Kool! Be cool!" And off we would go.

We managed to drive two miles before the car stalled in an intersection. It wasn't the first time, so I shouted my time-honored orders, "Hurry! Get out! Assume your positions!" Everyone spilled out of the car, laughing hysterically. My sisters pushed in back. I walked along the driver's side, guiding the steering wheel while pushing against the door frame.

"Do we keep going straight?" Linda yelled.

"Never straight! Always forward!" I yelled back

Straight, a term for someone who didn't smoke pot, was common jargon in the 1960s. Hip kids, like those of us living in Concord, used words like that.

***

I started smoking four months before my parents died because a popular girl in my high school class smoked. After three years of feeling like an outsider, I thought smoking would help me fit in. I'd wait until my parents went to bed, then sneak Dad's unfiltered Pall Malls from the fireplace mantle located a few steps from my bedroom.

The first time I smoked, I damn near passed out. We had a small bathroom in our bedroom with just enough room for a sink, mirror, toilet, and small square window. I grabbed the matchbook and cigarette hidden in my dresser drawer, took my grown-up paraphernalia into the bathroom, and shut the door.

I watched myself put the cigarette in my mouth and thought, *I look just like the movie stars on television.* After lighting the cigarette, I inhaled, then stood on my tippy toes to blow the smoke out the window. As soon as my feet were flat on the cold tile floor, my head began to swoon, and everything turned black. Horrified that I was dying, I flung open the bathroom door, threw myself on the bed, and laid there until the room stopped spinning. I lived, but my parents would have killed me if they found out.

Aunt Glo and Grandma Morris didn't care if I smoked. In fact, smoking Kools created a bond between Grandma and me. I took her to the store to buy cartons of cigarettes, and she paid me with a pack of smokes for giving her a lift. I smoked openly with Grandma and my uncle…cigarettes, that is. I smoked pot with Lee.

⤳

I met Lee on my first day at Pleasant Hill High School. When I was introduced as the new girl in class, she went out of her way to greet me. As luck would have it, we lived a block apart. We spent nearly every waking hour together, especially after school while her parents were at work. On short notice, Lee became my best friend and partner in crime.

Born and raised in the Bay Area, Lee embodied its culture—a poised free spirit skirting the edge of the hippie movement. She dressed the part, wearing suede jackets with fringe dangling from the sleeves, knee-high boots, and big hooped earrings. Lee was wise enough to not buck the establishment and savvy enough to dupe it.

Naturally pretty with pale porcelain skin, she wore little makeup. She had catlike blue eyes and thin blond hair that rested below her shoulders. Amiable and soft-spoken, her ethereal look and quiet demeanor cloaked the devil-may-care wild child that enjoyed drugs.

Our lives converged at a pivotal moment in time. I was dropped into the epicenter of the hippie counterculture where marijuana and psychedelics prevailed. With no adult supervision, I had the freedom to explore and the opportunity to reinvent myself. I was primed and ready. Underpinning it all, I ached to fill the void left by the death of my parents. It didn't take much coaxing from Lee to follow her lead.

She had access to drugs from a guy in a local band—at a cost, of course. Because she was attracted to him, she was more than happy to pay the price in exchange for free weed. We got stoned at least once a week at her house. Just before her parents came home, I would race down the street, run upstairs to my bedroom, and pretend to do my homework until I came down from my high.

One night in December 1968, I rushed home as I always did and pushed the door open to my bedroom. Inside were all my sisters. My startled expression did little to hide my altered state. My effort to avoid eye contact did not go unnoticed by Linda, the wannabe detective.

"You're stoned, aren't you, Kathi?" Linda asked while I fumbled for the Beatles' *White Album*.

"No! Why are you asking me that?" Keeping my head down, I lifted the acrylic lid on my most prized possession: a Pioneer record player.

"Yes, you are! Your eyes are all glossy and bloodshot!" My eyes were a dead giveaway every time I got high.

"Who cares? Sex, drugs, and rock and roll!" Usually paranoid when smoking weed, that day, I was fearless.

After placing the black vinyl record on the turntable and the needle carefully on its edge, I cranked up the volume. Carole sat beside me on the floor as we belted out every song.

The Beatles were my idols, and after the death of my parents, they became my roadmap.

Chapter 13

THE BEATLES

Sunday, February 9, 1964, the day the British invaded America, was a seminal moment in history and a day burned into our collective consciousness. For me, a thirteen-year-old in seventh grade, it was just another day living in San Jose. Chilly and overcast at 7:55 p.m., Janet, my friend next door, rang the doorbell.

"Kathi! Open the door!" she yelled through the windowpane.

Approaching the door from our hallway, I could see her through the glass, spinning like a top. As soon as I turned the knob, she pushed the door open and grabbed my hand. "Come on!" she ordered. "The show starts in five minutes!"

Confused, I asked, "What show?"

"Ed Sullivan!" she shouted as she pulled me out the door.

"So what?" Our family watched the show every Sunday night, but I never watched it with her.

"The Beatles are going to be on!"

"The beetles? Bugs? On *The Ed Sullivan Show*? What are you talking about?"

"No! Not bugs!" she laughed. "The band from England! The B.E.A.T.L.E.S! Beatles!"

"I have no idea who they are!"

"Well, everybody else does. Come on—we can't miss this! And just so you know, I've got dibs on John!"

We raced across the lawn toward her house when another friend from across the street stepped outside. "Pat! Hurry! It's starting! Follow us!"

Janet flung open her front door and led us into the living room. Plopping down on the hardwood floor, we sat crossed-legged in our pedal pushers just a few feet from the television. Her color console mahogany TV was far better than our black and white tabletop with rabbit ears. We watched intently as she turned the dial to CBS just in time for the show to start.

Ed Sullivan was America's Sunday night staple. Known for his stiff posture, deadpan face, and distinctive nasal accent, we never missed his "really big shew." When Ed announced, "Ladies and gentlemen— the Beatles," the camera panned to three guitarists and a drummer, all of them dressed in black suits, white shirts, skinny black ties, and mop-top haircuts.

During the broadcast, we learned their names were John, Paul, George, and Ringo. They didn't look anything like my heartthrobs: Paul Anka, Tony Curtis, and Ricky Nelson. Their first pop song, "All My Loving," didn't sound anything like my favorite music: Motown. I gravitated toward soul and rhythmic songs by artists like Smokey Robinson and the Miracles, Marvin Gaye, and Stevie Wonder.

They played five songs—each one whipped the audience of hysterical tweens into a bigger frenzy. Janet and Pat were right alongside them, screaming, "George! John! I love you!"

Unimpressed by them or their music, everyone's response baffled me. Especially because Janet had never mentioned the Beatles. How and when did she become a diehard fan?

An entire country was captivated by the lads from Liverpool that night. A record viewing audience of seventy-three million—60 percent of all televisions—tuned in. With a front-row seat to the birth of Beatlemania, it was apparent that I either join the hysteria or be an outcast. By the time they played their final song, "I Want to Hold Your Hand," yours truly was screaming, "Ringo! I love you!"

That night launched them on a meteoric rise to stardom. When they released their first movie in August 1964, *A Hard Day's Night*, I was first in line with Janet. Not because I was a Beatles fanatic like her. I tagged along because I agreed to anything to get out of the house.

Young and impressionable at fourteen years old, the lines of reality blurred in the intimacy of the dark theater that day. Captivated by their English accents, infectious personalities, and mischievous escapades, I fell in love. I believed every scene depicted who they genuinely were—fresh, honest, and unique. A devoted fan when the movie ended, I followed the Beatles like a cult from that day forward.

I babysat, saving every dime to buy all things Beatles: albums, magazines, dolls, and licorice records. I purchased John Lennon's book, *In His Own Write*, and covered every inch of my bedroom with posters and pages from magazines. Obsessed, I dreamt about marrying Ringo and our life together.

As the 1960s continued and the Beatles evolved, I watched them from the sidelines. Their mop tops grew long and disheveled.

Fitted suits were replaced with psychedelic bellbottoms and fur vests. Innocent, sweet songs like "I Want to Hold Your Hand" mutated to mind-altering songs like "Lucy in the Sky with Diamonds," though the Beatles denied that it spoke to LSD (still, the acronym points to it).

After my parents died, I searched for meaning and direction and found it with the Beatles. At a time when I needed someone to hold my hand, I held theirs. In a world deaf to my pain, music spoke the loudest—music like the lyrics in "Blackbird" on their *White Album*. While living at my aunts, I made a conscious decision to follow their lead to turn on, tune in, and drop out.

Chapter 14

REVOLUTION

While I was getting stoned with Lee, unbeknownst to me, my cousin Brad was also getting high. Unfortunately for us both, we got busted on the same day. He got off with a scolding while I got grounded. Irritated that he been caught and reprimanded, he pushed Linda as he made his way downstairs.

Judy was furious that Brad and I did not receive the same punishment, and that no action was taken against him for pushing Linda. She wrote a letter to her boyfriend in Madera detailing how we were not treated the same and that our aunt was not in compliance with court orders. She added that she hated living at our aunt's as much as she hated living in Concord.

Judy gave the letter to Aunt Glo and asked her to mail it on her way to work. Sometime that day, our aunt spotted our cousin's name through the envelope, opened it, and read the contents. When she returned home from work, all hell broke loose. After lashing out at Judy for telling the truth, she unleashed a battery of regrets and admonishments on the rest of us. Judy tried to talk to her, but our aunt refused to speak or even look at her.

All ten of us protested by taking refuge in my bedroom. We refused to leave the room for any reason, including meals. Our rebellion was the straw that broke the camel's back. We lived with our aunt and uncle for less than five months. Our short stay included three birthdays, Halloween, Thanksgiving, and Christmas. I don't remember celebrating any of them.

In the middle of January 1969, we piled into the same Volkswagen bus that carried us to Concord and returned to the Central Valley. In the middle of the night, our aunt and uncle unceremoniously dumped us in our grandparent's driveway and sped away.

It may not have been the best recommendation by the Madera Probation Department to place ten Catholic children with a non-religious couple—a working couple enjoying a sedate life and lazy weekends on their houseboat christened PAX, the Latin word for "peace." A couple who, until our parents were killed, had not fostered or expressed a desire for more children.

Perhaps a wealthy Catholic couple desiring a larger family would be a better fit.

Chapter 15

PIT STOP

When our uncle drove onto our grandparents' driveway, reporters sprang from cars parked on the street. Their ambush caught us off guard—it was late evening and dark outside. Pressing their black cameras to the windows on both sides of the Volkswagen bus, their flashbulbs blinded us as they snapped pictures from every angle.

We were surprised because we didn't expect them. I was irritated because I thought our newsworthiness ended when we were sent to live with Aunt Glo. I exclaimed out loud to nobody in particular, "Why are they here? How did they know we were coming?"

Our uncle left the car running as we unloaded the few clothes we brought and pushed the door shut. It was a matter-of-fact, unemotional parting with no tears, hugs, or drawn-out farewells.

I bolted up the cement porch steps and pounded on the front door of our grandparent's house. Grandma opened it, her steely blue eyes smiling through her glasses. It was always unnerving for me to look at her because when I stared into my grandmother's face, I saw my mother.

"Kackie! You made it!" Grandma's pet name for me felt comforting. My nickname was created years earlier because the little kids couldn't pronounce the "th" in Kathi. Extending her arms, she drew me in to hug her. Grandma was short, only 5'2", like my mother. Her Chantilly dusting powder reached me before she did.

"Grandma! Do you know there are reporters outside?"

"No, I had no idea." She turned on the porch light, pushed the screen door open, and rotated her head in all directions.

"Well, there are, and I'm not talking to any of them! How did they know we were coming?"

"I don't know. Now get inside before you catch a cold!"

Grandma stood at the door and hugged each of my siblings as they filed in. With no love lost between my aunt and uncle and grandparents, the adults did not greet one another. Once we unloaded, our aunt and uncle backed up and drove away.

⌁

My grandparents' home that they bought in the late 1940s was the one steady constant in our lives. Whereas our family moved frequently, Grandma and Grandpa stayed put in their little house on Hedges Avenue.

That night, the first time we had been back since the accident, was disturbing. While my grandmother talked to me, I was lost in images. Pictures played in my mind, like someone describing a near-death experience when their lives flash before them. I didn't hear a word she said. All I saw were a lifetime of memories at my grandparents' house.

⤙

Memories of crisp autumn days and the sturdy maple tree in front of their house. The orange and yellow leaves, some as big as our heads, blanketed the lawn and street when they dropped. Grandpa would rake them into a massive pile and set them ablaze. Brandishing his Chicago accent with a topping of Lithuanian, he'd yell, "Hey, yous! Yeah, yous—you little shootusses! Don't go near the fire!" Sounding gruff to strangers, we knew it was all love, as was the comforting smell of the burning leaves.

We spent lazy afternoons climbing the tall almond and walnut trees in their backyard, picking some of the nuts for Grandma's baking and most of them for our bellies. On hot summer days, we walked seven miles to and from Blakeley's public swimming pool and stopped along the way to pick loquats from low-hanging branches. Our minds focused on our destination kept us from keeling over in the blistering sun.

For the fifty cents entrance fee, we spent the afternoon slathered in Coppertone suntan lotion, strutting our stuff and checking out the guys. Tunes like "Surf City," "It's My Party," and "Sugar Shack" blasted over the loudspeaker. The double metal slide was screaming mad fun and the diving tower, over two stories high, separated the men from the boys.

When we returned home from our hot, exhausting walk, we made a mad dash to the swamp cooler mounted in the dining room window. All of us took turns lifting our shirts and sighing with pleasure as the cool, wet air blew against our sweaty skin.

Later that night, we sat in the backyard on yellow Adirondack chairs, torturing slugs. After covering them with salt, we marveled at how they bubbled in their feeble attempt to slither away. When they lost their fight and melted like the wicked witch in *The Wizard of Oz*, nature retaliated by sending ginormous June bugs to terrorize us. Our girlish screams filled the night.

The best memory of all was our magical and joyful Christmas celebrations with our grandparents, aunts, uncles, and cousins. When we entered the house, the scent of pine needles laced with the aromatic baking ham welcomed us to the festivities. Thirty of us would cram into our grandparent's small home and thought nothing of it. The Christmas tree that Grandma meticulously decorated with vintage Shiney Brite ornaments, tinsel, and lights that bubbled, sat proudly in the bay window. Under the tree were beautifully wrapped gifts for everyone. We searched the packages, looking for our names, and groaned when our parents told us to not pick them up.

Everyone looked forward to the food served only at Christmas. Ham, sausage, and hot German potato salad. Desserts were my favorite: pumpkin bread, decadent chocolate fudge, and three-layered Jell-O.

Grandma played the piano while we gathered around her singing Christmas carols. The wooden metronome kept time while we fought to sit beside her on the piano bench. At midnight we sang "Happy Birthday" to Jesus and let the youngest blow out the single candle on the yule log-shaped cake.

One year, I swore I saw Santa's sleigh and reindeer flying over the rooftops.

↵

The night we were dumped at my grandparents was like viewing my past and present life through an altered lens. In front of me—my grandparents who loved us. Behind me—my aunt and uncle who wanted us gone. Above me—somewhere in Heaven, my parents who I missed with an ever-present ache. A disemboweled void shared only by those who have lost a loved one. My hollowness multiplied with the loss of two.

My grandparents' house was familiar and comforting. For seventeen years it was our one constant. It was a single-story square-shaped home. The front door opened into the living room, which had plastered walls painted pale green and green shag carpet. An arched opening separated the living room from the dining room. The dining room was just large enough for a table with six chairs.

A mahogany Baldwin piano placed along the living room's back wall was the first thing one noticed when entering. Pictures of The Last Supper and a black panther crouching on a tree branch hung on the walls, and a cream-colored sofa was tucked inside the bay window.

The galley-style kitchen, adjacent to the dining room, was narrow and had a window over the kitchen sink that faced the backyard. The left side of the house had two bedrooms separated by a bath.

On the dining room wall hung a picture collage of all the grandchildren, with my picture at the top. It made me feel special when Grandma said with a twinkle in her eye, "Don't tell the others, but you are my favorite first grandchild."

⟿

When I finished talking to Grandma in the living room, my sisters followed me into the kitchen.

"Did you see the guy parked in front of the Larsons' house? As soon as we passed him, he jumped out of his car and ran to the bus!"

Linda's hazel eyes were on fire as she waved her arm, demonstrating how he flung the door open.

"No, I didn't see anything until a camera was two inches from my face. I still see spots from his stupid flashbulb!" Judy blinked while smoothing her cotton blouse with both hands.

We were still comparing notes when the doorbell rang. Linda poked her head around the kitchen corner to see who it was. Her short light brown hair dangled to the side while she hung on to the door jamb.

"It's a couple of those reporters...and Grandma is letting them in!" Linda said.

"What is she thinking? I'm not talking to anybody!" Judy snarled.

"I already told her that!" I assured her.

We remained in the kitchen and listened to Grandma's cheerful and animated conversation that lasted close to ten minutes. When she called out, "Kathi, come here, please," I shook my head, threw my hands in the air, and mouthed to my sisters, "I'm going to kill her."

In the living room, standing next to the piano, were two reporters and Grandma. They had their backs turned to me. As I circled around, I was startled to see Grandma beaming like a schoolgirl invited to her first dance. *She's enjoying all this attention! I bet she's the one that told them we were coming!*

"Kathi, this nice man would like to talk to you." Her voice was coquettish—three octaves higher than usual.

Reaching into a black work bag draped on his shoulder, the reporter pulled out a pen and notepad. Smiling, he turned toward me and said, "Hi Kathi, if you don't mind, I'd like to ask you a few questions."

"I'm sorry, but I am not giving interviews anymore. I really wish you guys would leave us alone."

Grandma's jaw dropped. The reporter's dejected look made me sad for a split second. I returned to the kitchen with my sisters proud of the backbone I had sprouted. It was the last time we saw the media.

We stayed with our grandparents for a few days until the court found a foster home to place us in. The foster family met us in our grandparent's living room for simple introductions and polite handshakes as we shared names and ages. Rushed and awkward, the move happened quickly.

Not unlike my stay.

Chapter 16

FOSTER HOME TWO

Aunt Glo's modern, avant-garde house couldn't hold a candle to the classic elegance and old-world charm of our second foster home. Located in an affluent area of Fresno, the four thousand square foot Spanish-style home was nothing short of spectacular.

Built in 1940, the two-story home had five bedrooms, three and a half baths with another free-standing half bath in the backyard. A three-car garage, sixteen hundred square foot basement, and wine cellar. Hardwood floors, mahogany staircase, and built-in butler's pantry. Three fireplaces. The fireplace in the living room was encased with a marble mantle, hearth, and Corinthian columns.

Every room was massive, with crown molding and lofty ceilings. Bedrooms the size of dorms. The wine cellar the size of a small bedroom. Elegant and vintage Victorian furniture with ornate carvings in dark wood. Heavy luxurious fabrics covered the windows.

Aunt Glo's home, although a step up from what we were used to, felt normal. The second foster home felt like a palace. And as sensational as it was, nothing was inviting about it.

Their car, a white Cadillac with a plush white leather interior, was like riding in a celestial cloud. A far cry from our aunt and uncle's Volkswagen bus or the cars we had grown up with.

The foster mother, Alice, was pregnant, a stay-at-home mom, and had two children from her first marriage. Her husband was a traveling salesman and stocked sunglasses in department stores. Together they had a set of twin boys.

The day we arrived, they enrolled us in Catholic schools. We older girls took the bus to San Joaquin Memorial High school. St. Therese, a block away, was close enough for the younger ones to walk to school and all of us to walk to Mass. Their resume for the court was developing nicely. For us—another story.

Alice and I soon learned we did not see eye to eye. My first serious conversation with her occurred within a few weeks of our arrival.

"Kathi, please sit with me." She led me to a couple of chairs and a marble table in the living room, next to a window that faced the street.

"I've been thinking. I understand you will be turning eighteen next month, correct?"

"Yes. I am," I replied.

"How would you like to be a debutante?"

"What's a debutante?" I had never heard the word.

"It's a formal ball where you are introduced to society."

"Who would be there?"

"Our family, friends, and neighbors, along with past debutantes."

I had visions of mean rich girls grouped together, whispering and ridiculing me, the shy girl. The one who tried to hide under the school desk so as not to be the center of attention. I wanted no part of being the belle of the ball. Instead of joy, I felt distressed. Alice wanted me to instantly transition into her world, where I had no idea what to expect or how to act.

"No, that is not something I would be interested in at all."

"Don't you think it would be fun to go shopping together? We could take a trip to San Francisco and pick out a beautiful gown. You could wear my diamond earrings and necklace."

"Well, that might be fun, but I don't want to be at a party with a bunch of people I don't know."

She stood up, squinted as she looked down at me, and said, "Okay, I can't force you. But I think you will regret this decision." Then stomped away with her nose in the air.

Another incident occurred in the kitchen. I was sitting on the wooden bench at the long farmhouse table, watching her fry hamburgers. She turned her head to look at me and asked, "How on earth did your mother feed twelve people? I know your family didn't have a lot of money."

Not sure how to answer—we ate three meals a day—I asked, "What do you mean?"

"What kind of meals did your mother prepare?"

"Spaghetti, hotdogs, chili beans. Sometimes we had pancakes." They were all typical dinners, as far as I knew.

"I don't know how she did it!" Her voice trailed as she turned back around.

Perplexed, I continued to watch her. I had no problem cooking for twelve. What was the problem cooking for sixteen? Was it the amount of work? It certainly couldn't be the money. She lived in a castle—four of our homes could fit into her one. Besides, they received social security payments for each of us, totaling six hundred and fifty dollars a month (equivalent to four thousand seven hundred dollars in 2020 money).

The last encounter occurred in my bedroom. We four oldest girls shared a room with an attached bath. I had just completed decorating the room with magazine pictures, probably of the Beatles, when Alice walked in. Looking around, she began to cry as she held me by the shoulders and said, "Thank you! It's beautiful!"

Confused, I responded, "You're welcome." *There's nothing beautiful about it. All I did was tape some pictures to the wall. Why is she crying?*

It was evident she was struggling to cope. On occasion, she asked me about our family life and seemed disturbed when I told her how much I helped around the house and with my siblings. I know she was resentful because she said, "You took care of the kids; they all look to you." When I offered advice on how to interact with or discipline my siblings, it landed on deaf ears. The underlying message was clear: your siblings will not listen to me, and I refuse to listen to you.

And then there was her husband—the arrogant tyrannical militant. Tall, over six feet, he looked like Lurch in the television show *The Addams Family*, so that's what we called him. He had a long face with deep-set eyes and sandy blond hair combed forward. He didn't walk; he strutted like a haughty rooster. He didn't talk; he lectured and pontificated.

Within a brief time, I realized all of us were struggling. I felt invisible and fell into a downward spiral at rocket speed. I don't remember specifics as much as I remember the feeling of despair. It affected me to the point that I cannot remember the names, ages, or faces of their children. In my mind's eye, they don't exist because I cannot see them.

The sense of abandonment, a constant companion since losing my parents, was heaped with hopelessness at that foster home. It felt like a forced existence in an aristocratic fortress. I wondered if I would ever be happy again.

Despite it all, I looked forward to my birthday. Our mother made a point of making our day special. With our large family, it was easy to get lost in the crowd. So, birthday parties, where we were the main attraction, were treasured celebrations we looked forward to all year long. Mom baked and decorated a cake or bought sheet cakes from the bakery with flowers and fancy edging. She would make our favorite dinner and gather the family together as we opened our gifts.

I hoped my eighteenth birthday might turn things around. It was when Alice suggested I become a debutante. Surely, she would do something to make the day special for me.

On Friday, the day before my birthday, Aunt Mary took me to a pizza parlor after school. Lurch happened to be home that day. As soon as I walked in, his booming voice asked, "Where have you been? It's 4:15. You know you're supposed to be home at 4:00."

"Aunt Mary took me to Me-N-Ed's." I couldn't believe how angry he was over a mere fifteen minutes.

"You're late!" He towered over me as he spat his words.

"I'm sorry. She just wanted to do something for my birthday." We were standing near the staircase in the foyer. I backed up to give space between him and me.

"None of that matters! You're grounded for a week!"

That was it. Nothing was premeditated. I was just done.

I sprinted upstairs to the bathroom in our bedroom, opened the medicine cabinet that hung over the sink, and scanned the pills. There were lots of bottles. Allergy pills. Aspirin. No-Doz. I didn't think any of them alone would kill me. I thought if I took enough of all of them, they might.

I spilled aspirin into my hand. Put the pills in my mouth. Turned on the faucet, cupped my hand for water, threw back my head, and swallowed. Next came the No-Doz, followed by the allergy pills. I was deciding what to take next when I heard someone enter the bedroom. Just as I slammed the medicine door shut, my sister Linda stepped up behind me.

"What are you doing?" Her voice was thick with concern.

"Nothing! Go away!" I ordered and turned to push her.

"Yes, you are! You're taking pills! I saw you!" She gripped my shoulders and tried to pull me out of the bathroom. "Kathi! Stop it!" She begged.

I grabbed hold of the sink, "Leave me alone! Go downstairs and mind your own business!" No match for her strength; she grabbed my arm and pulled me into the bedroom.

"Help! Somebody come here!" Linda yelled.

"What is going on?" I could hear Alice's footsteps down the hall.

"I just saw Kathi take a bunch of pills!"

"Oh, my God! What did you take? Linda, run and get Doctor Pardini! Hurry!"

Dr. Pardini lived directly across the street. He arrived within minutes, asked what I took, and checked my vitals. Although he assured me that I would be fine, he told the foster parents to keep me awake. I spent the evening lying and shivering on the sofa in the living room, surrounded by my siblings. My ten-year-old brother Mike sat on the floor close to my head and checked on me every few minutes. The smile on his face did not conceal the concern in his eyes.

The next day, my eighteenth birthday, Lurch said I would have to leave. He and his wife were not interested in fostering a troubled teen turned adult. With my attempted suicide, he believed I would be a bad influence on their kids and my siblings.

I packed my clothes and said my goodbyes. I had just reached the front door when little Eddie ran to me with his arms lifted in the air. As soon as I picked him up, he wrapped his arms tight around my neck.

"I love you, Kackie."

"I love you too, Eddie."

At seventeen, I lost my parents.

At eighteen, I lost my brothers and sisters.

Chapter 17

I THOUGHT JESUS DIED FOR GIRLS LIKE ME

I stayed with my grandparents while a social worker, Grandma, and I debated where to place me. It didn't register that when I turned eighteen, I became an adult and didn't need their approval. Still, as an unemployed orphaned high school student, I had few options.

We agreed it was important to graduate from the school I was enrolled in, San Joaquin Memorial High School (SJM). In my third high school, with three months left of my senior year, I did not want to enroll in a fourth high school.

We disagreed on where I should live. My preference was the Young Women's Christian Association in downtown Fresno. Grandma made it clear it was not an option for the exact reason I wanted to live there: no supervision. Her choice was the boarding house at SJM, the same boarding house where my fourteen-year-old mother lived when my grandparents moved from Illinois to California. Ultimately, Grandma won the debate.

The boarding house was located on the same property as the school. Farmhouse style, two-story, with white siding and a green dormer on top, it had red brick stairs leading to a spacious covered porch supported by several white beams. Taking up residence required screening and approval from the Franciscan nuns who lived there, particularly Mother Superior.

The day I arrived, she met me at the door dressed in a full black habit and invited me into the living room. A hefty woman with a kind face, she tried to put me at ease. Although I no longer feared nuns, they still intimidated me.

The large, sparsely furnished room had hardwood floors. Several large windows covered with white mini blinds allowed plenty of natural light. An area rug anchored the two oversized sofas that faced each other. A console television sat in one corner, and in the opposite corner, double glass doors led into a den.

The only bedroom on the first floor was in the corner to the left of the front door. It was small, with just enough space for two twin beds, a dresser, a wooden desk, and a chair. Two doors flanked opposite ends of the room. One accessed the den and the other the living room. Like the living room, large windows lined both walls. It soon became my room.

Mother Superior invited me to sit beside her on the red patterned sofa. "I am Mother Superior, but you may call me Mother Terese. Besides the nuns, we have two other girls living here—Niko and Doris. Niko is a senior and a foreign exchange student from Japan. Doris is a sophomore. Her family lives in Yosemite."

Mother Terese asked me questions centered around responsibility, independence, and aspirations. During our conversation, she stopped mid-sentence to say she had never met anyone with eyes as expressive as mine. Her eyes were pale blue and kind. They reminded me of my grandmother's.

A half-hour into the interview, she reached into the folds of her black habit and pulled out a key. "Kathi, I think you will be a wonderful addition to our home. I'm so impressed with your maturity that I am giving you a key to the front door. No other girl has received this privilege."

Surprised and honored, I moved in that day.

Living on campus had its perks. I put on my makeup, got dressed, and drank coffee until the bell rang, with ample time to reach class. With no one to buy me clothes, wearing uniforms was a blessing. I didn't have to worry about competing with classmates' outfits. Hiking up our blue and green plaid skirts or wearing white knee-high socks was the only way to stand out.

Under different conditions, living at the boarding house would have been enjoyable. It lent itself to the one thing I longed for most— freedom! I was not under the watchful eye of anyone. Other than the requirement to ask permission to leave and return by curfew, I was unsupervised.

The downside was that the boarding house introduced me to painful separation, deafening silence, and loneliness. I looked forward to school where I could interact with people. I saw my sisters on campus, but we had little time to talk. I dreaded school dismissal because when I returned home, it was to solitary confinement.

For eighteen years, I had been surrounded by family, noise, and activity. All of us were always busy doing something. If not chores, we played board games such as Monopoly or Life, or card games such as War or Oh Hell. We played records and danced together. The little kids had the big kids as tutors for their homework. We fed, changed, and played with the babies as if they were our dolls. The older girls rolled each other's hair. We sat at the dining room table, said grace, and ate meals together. We fought, laughed, and gossiped. All of it was comforting. It meant we belonged. It meant home.

The boarding house did not feel like a home. There was no interaction among any of us. We girls went to school and did our homework in our rooms. On the weekends, Doris returned to her family in Yosemite, and Niko visited her host family. I seldom saw the nuns and don't know how many lived there. Instead of using the front door to come and go, they used the back entrance.

I was alone on the first floor and did not have a roommate. The other girls and all the nun's bedrooms were upstairs. The living room outside my bedroom door, with nothing more than sofas and a television, served more as a pass-through than a gathering place.

The kitchen separated our cafeteria-style dining room from the nun's dining room. A Dutch door led into the kitchen. The upper half of the door opened; the bottom half had a wide shelf. The cook placed our food on the shelf, then closed the top half. It felt like a prison cell where an inmate's food is passed under the door. Often, I ate alone.

Despite limited encounters, my perception of cantankerous nuns remained unchanged. Once, Niko and I accompanied several of them on a day trip to Yosemite. They weren't the least bit friendly or talkative on the long three-hour drive. When we reached Yosemite and parked the van, they offered us coffee and donuts. When I asked for sugar for my coffee, one of them snapped, "Take a bite out of a donut!

Then drink your coffee! The sugar in your mouth will sweeten it! That's all the sugar you need!"

On another occasion, Doris and I were watching television. A commercial with girls on a beach wearing bikinis was playing when a nun entered the living room. With disgust written all over her face, she stomped to the television and changed the channel. "You girls should not be watching that! It's too risqué!" Doris and I rolled our eyes and covered our mouths to muffle our laughter.

I had very few visitors. Dad's cousin stopped by occasionally to bring me toiletries. My grandparents and siblings visited once, a month after I moved in, on Easter Sunday. My pacing wore a trail on the front lawn as I waited for them that afternoon.

⌁

Growing up, Easter was a celebration with family. Mom went out of her way to make the day, and all of us, feel special. We spent Saturday afternoon dying dozens of eggs for the Easter bunny to hide throughout the house. Mom stayed up half the night filling our baskets with candy, stuffed animals, and small toys like jacks and silly putty. Sunday morning, everyone raced to find the eggs and their Easter baskets.

I didn't mind getting ready for church on Easter because Mom bought us new outfits from head to toe. Shiny patent leather shoes and socks with ruffles as a young girl; white pumps and nylons as a teenager. Lacy white underwear, bloomers, and silk slips that felt good against my skin. White gloves, hats, and purses. One of the most memorable outfits was when we five oldest girls wore matching pink chiffon dresses with black velvet trim and layers of taffeta petticoats.

Mom and Dad led their parade down the church aisle like a proud lion and lioness with their cubs. After Mass, we returned home to Easter brunch. The potato salad, made with our dyed Easter eggs, looked festive with its specks of colors—purple, pink, and green. We gorged on jellybeans and egg-shaped chocolate-covered marshmallows while playing jacks and lifting the print off newspapers with the silly putty.

$\backsim$

Easter 1969 was the first holiday that I spent alone. My grandparents brought my brothers and sisters to the boarding house just long enough for the big kids to hide some eggs, the little kids to find them and leave. There was no all-day holiday celebration. No feast or Easter basket filled with candy. No new outfit and Mass with my family. I spent the day lying in bed, crying for happy memories slipping away.

I was never offered therapy despite losing my parents, my siblings, and attempting suicide. Things were different in the 1960s; counseling was not provided like it is today. Still, out of human compassion, I thought someone would try to console and comfort me. Especially the nuns.

One night, while I laid in bed weeping, Mother Terese's sister, the cook and maid (who was not a nun), heard me through the door. She knocked, entered, and asked, "Kathi, what's wrong?"

She sat on my bed and stroked my hair.

"I miss my mom and dad. I miss my brothers and sisters. I feel so alone."

"You're breaking my heart. I wish there was something I could do," she said while choking back tears and continuing to plead. When my sobs softened to whimpers, she left. There was nothing she could do for an orphan in hellish isolation with icy nuns.

〜

Despite my living conditions and loneliness, my roommates and I were able to grab a few laughs on occasion. One day Niko mentioned she liked a Japanese rice wine called Sake. Doris and I decided to surprise her with a bottle. I don't remember who we bribed to buy it, but I do remember it was a big mistake.

On a beautiful sunny afternoon, I ran into Niko as we made our way up the steps of the boarding house. "Niko! I have a surprise for you!"

"A surprise? For me? I don't understand."

"I can't tell you, or it won't be a surprise! Meet Doris and me in the den at 7:00 sharp!"

As luck would have it, several nuns decided to watch television in the living room that night. A set of double glass doors separated the living room from the den. The three of us girls said hello to the nuns as we strolled casually across the living room and shut the glass doors behind us. Doris had the bottle hidden in her purse. We turned the radio station to KYNO and sat cross-legged on the hardwood floor. Our backs were toward the glass doors and prevented the nuns from seeing our contraband centered between us.

Doris reached into her purse, grabbed the top of the bottle, and inched it into view. "Sake!" Niko exclaimed as her eyes darted from Doris to me and back again.

"Go ahead, Niko! Take the first drink!" Doris handed her the bottle.

Niko took a sip.

"So good! I love Sake! I haven't had it since I left Japan. Here try some!" she said, and handed the bottle to me.

I drank beer once at Millerton Lake with a group of friends. It was a hot sizzling summer afternoon and my lily-white skin was fried red. On the way home, I vomited all over the passenger side of the cute guy's car.

A month later at a house party, some of my friends offered me a Coors Light. When I declined, asserting that my short-lived drinking career had ended at the lake, they assured me that I would acquire a taste for beer if I continued to drink. "Why would I want to do that? It tastes like piss, and it made me sick!"

It turned out that Sake wasn't much better. After a disgusting swig, I handed the bottle back to her and said, "It's all yours." At which point, Niko leaned her head back and gulped some more of the wine.

"I don't think that's a good idea," Doris warned her. But the damage had been done. Her face, with its shit-eating grin, began to flush.

"Niko! You're turning red!" I exclaimed in horror.

Laughing uncontrollably, she responded, "I know, it happens when I drink."

I yanked the bottle away and tried to reason with her. "Oh, my God! You can't have any more! We're all going to get into so much trouble!"

Niko, immersed in the sweet seduction of her homeland wine, wrestled it away and finished off the bottle. Soon we had our hands full with an intoxicated red-faced laughing hyena. As hard as we tried, there was no silencing her.

"We have to get her out of the house before we get busted!" Doris said while covering Niko's mouth with her hand.

"I know, but we have to go through the front door with the nuns sitting right there!" I said.

"They have their backs to us. Let's hold her up and go through your room. Let me do the talking when we get to the front door," Doris said, then glared at Niko. "Niko, do not say a word!" Doris's stern command had little effect.

Doris and I stood her up, draped her arms over our shoulders, and muscled our stocky drunken roommate to the front door. "We're going to get some fresh air!" Doris chirped to the nuns through a forced smile.

We dragged Niko down the steps to the baseball diamond across the street. Eventually, her laughing ceased, and her demeanor turned from hysterics to insisting on laying in the field to take a nap. It was a close call, and one not repeated at the boarding house. Outside of the house was a different story.

As graduation approached, the rite of passage from high school to college kicked into full swing. Our senior class of two hundred was small enough for everyone to know each other, and large enough to garner decent-sized parties involving alcohol. Many were house parties; others were in the country around huge bonfires, but I was more interested in boys than liquor. The only time I got busted was on Senior Ditch Day. A group of us making out on the white sands of Carmel beach missed the boarding call and delayed the bus trip home. Aside from that incident, I kept Mother Terese's trust by checking in by my midnight curfew.

⤙

In June 1969, three months after my removal from the second foster home, my siblings were placed in a third foster home in Madera. The newspapers stated that the basis for the move was Alice's ill health. Ill health, I believe, translated to stress. Pregnant Alice, with four children of her own, realized she bit off more than she could chew. I found it interesting that, like our aunt, five months of fostering was the breaking point.

My siblings lived in the third foster home for a week before my high school graduation. I met their new foster parents when they brought my siblings to the Fresno Convention Center for the ceremony. I was grateful until I heard the little kids talking to them.

In the lobby, I pulled Judy aside. "What is going on? I just heard Mike call her mom!"

"I know. I'm mad too," Judy said. "As soon as we moved in, they said we had to call them Mom and Dad. Don't worry, none of us big kids have any intention of ever calling them that."

I left them and made my way to the stage. After taking my chair, I looked out into the sea of faces, acutely aware that my mom and dad were not in the audience. I watched my classmates scan the crowd, and their faces light up when they spotted their parents. They waved wildly while their families yelled their names and waved back with matched enthusiasm—a milestone celebration with graduates and their parents. For me, it was one more merciless reminder that I didn't have any.

After the ceremony, we had a school-sanctioned all-night party at Belmont Country Club. I mingled for a few hours, then left with a group of friends and a well-known stoner named Scott.

We crammed into the backseat of Scott's car. He turned and asked, "Which one of you clowns knows how to roll a joint?"

"I do!" one of the guys answered, then reached inside his jacket. "I've got papers and a pipe too! Just pass me the weed!"

Scott tossed him a baggie and said, "Let's go to the cemetery and spin donuts!" He started the car and pushed a Creedence Clearwater eight-track into the tape player. We shared a joint while Scott drove eleven miles west to the Belmont Memorial Cemetery. All of us, stoned stupid, sang "Suzie Q" at the top of our lungs. Once inside, our vocals turned to screams as Scott cranked the wheel and spun the car—all of us holding on for dear life.

When we left the cemetery, it was well after midnight. With nothing to do but look for trouble, we headed to Sin City—blocks of apartments near Fresno State College occupied by college students. Scott knew of a party with SJM alumni.

As soon as we entered the apartment, I fell in lust with a blue-eyed blond named Dan. Not my usual type, I preferred dark hair and eyes—but there was something about the way he looked at me that drew me in. Nothing happened that night other than us graduating seniors trying to act grown up drinking and smoking pot. We returned to our all-night party at the country club in time to get picked up by unsuspecting adults.

A week later, my girlfriend and I drove to Dan's apartment for another party. He and his friends liked to drink, smoke hash, and take psychedelics. That night they were taking mescaline and urged me to join them. It took some coercing because I was known as a lightweight. Although I smoked pot, I was not fond of alcohol and had never taken psychedelics. Eventually, I caved and took the pill because I didn't want Dan to think I was an immature little girl just out of high school.

It didn't take long to feel the effects of the drug. Dan's good friend Marshall—gorgeous, with a head of thick, shiny black hair—sat across from me at the dining room table.

"Do you want to do something that feels incredible?"

"Maybe. What is it?" I asked coyly.

"Here, straddle this chair." He pushed a kitchen chair toward me. "Sit down, lean over, and press the top of your head to the top of mine. Close your eyes and follow my lead."

It didn't take much convincing for me to want to touch Marshall. Together we rotated the tops of our heads in long, slow circular motions. The sensation, as if our souls melded into one, was intense and sensual. Transported to a place of ecstasy, basking in pleasure, I didn't want the feeling to end.

As midnight approached, my girlfriend nudged me and broke the spell. "Kathi, we have to get you home!" When I sat up, the head rush, unexpected and extraordinary, left me craving more.

"I don't want to go!"

"You have to. You know you're going to get in trouble by Mother Terese if you don't."

"Dan, will you guys take me home and then wait for me in the parking lot? I just need to check-in. Once everyone's in bed, I will jump out the window. I promise it won't be more than five or ten minutes."

Dan and his buddies drove me home and parked in the lot adjacent to the boarding house. I pointed to the window in the den. "That's the window I'm going to jump out of. Promise me you'll wait."

When I entered the house, Mother Terese came downstairs, said good night, and locked the door. I watched her walk upstairs, then went into my bedroom, shut the door, and laid on my bed. While I was staring at the Beatles poster taped to the door, Ringo started to move.

"Whoa! What the hell?" I murmured out loud to myself. Nobody warned me that I would see things. While I continued to trip on the poster with colors melding and flowing like a river, the door suddenly opened. Niko had decided, for the first time ever, to pay me a midnight visit.

"Niko! What are you doing in here?"

"I waited up for you. I want to hear how your night went with Dan."

"It was fabulous! But I'm exhausted. I will tell you all about it in the morning, okay?"

Rather than leave, she knelt down beside me. Her eyes opened wide when she looked into mine.

"Kathi...what is wrong with you?"

"Nothing!"

"Your eyes! They looked scared!"

"Niko, I am fine. Please, just leave." My agitation rose by the second.

"No, something is wrong. Your eyes." She leaned in close.

"Be quiet! If Mother Terese comes down here, I will be so mad at you!"

"I think I need to tell Mother! You aren't acting right!"

"Oh my God, Niko, if you say anything to her, I will never talk to you again! Look, I took something, but I'll be fine. Now go to your room. I will see you in the morning."

I grew more and more nervous, fearing the guys would leave, and I knew better than to tell Niko they were waiting.

After several minutes of arguing, she finally left. I tiptoed into the den, lifted the window, pushed open the screen, and jumped three feet to the ground.

By the time I reached the car, my heart was pounding like a jack-hammer. When I opened the door and sat down, fear shot through me.

"What took you so long?" Dan asked. "We were getting ready to leave."

"I couldn't get Niko out of my room, and now I'm freaking out."

They explained to me that I was simply feeling the effect of the drug. To help calm me down, they told jokes and drove the streets of Fresno. Eventually I relaxed, but I was no longer in the mood to party. They weren't interested in babysitting me either, so when I asked them to take me home, they were happy to oblige. I used the key to the front door that Mother Terese had entrusted me with and slipped inside—smug that I had gotten away with my midnight caper.

The following day I had a date for the movies. To leave the boarding house for any reason required approval from Mother Terese. She was sitting in the living room when I approached her.

"Mother Terese, is it okay if I go to the movies tonight? Hank will be here to pick me up at seven."

"Kathi, I have something I need to discuss with you. Brother John came to see me this morning. He said last night when he and the brothers were on a midnight stroll, they saw someone jump out the window. Was that you?"

"Yes." *I can't believe this.*

"Why would you do such a thing?"

"I was at a party, and I didn't want to leave."

"Do you understand you put our lives in jeopardy? We can't have girls like you living here. I will be calling your grandmother to tell her that new living arrangements need to be made immediately. Now go to the chapel and pray for forgiveness. When you are done praying, pack your things and clean your room. Scrub the floor and all the window blinds."

I took my time walking to the chapel, knelt, and thought about everything but prayer. *You can't have girls like me living here? Because I'm a sinner? Aren't nuns married to Jesus, who came to earth to save sinners? I thought Jesus died for girls like me!*

I understood I deserved to be punished because I had broken the rules. I felt terrible that I disappointed her and lost her trust. Still, I was angry and hurt at how easily she dismissed me.

Mother Terese allowed me to stay at the boarding house while a social worker, a psychiatrist, and Grandma Lachawicz deliberated on where to place me. When I told them that I wanted to move back to Aunt Glo's, Grandma Lachawicz resisted. She referred to Aunt Glo as the "red-headed bitch." Because of her objection, the social worker took me to a psychiatrist who had me complete a twelve-page psychiatric evaluation. The results were that I was normal and used to getting my own way. Although I had no doubt that I was normal, to say I was used to getting my own way was bizarre. My mother had ruled with a heavy hand. As the oldest, I was definitely the bossiest with my siblings. But it was a different story with authority figures. I was a shrinking violet and compliant.

When the ten of us were awarded to Aunt Glo, the plan was for me to graduate from high school and enroll in a community college near our aunts' house—Diablo Valley College. I loved living in Concord and I enjoyed the short time that I lived with my aunt; however, because she had shipped us out after five months, the social worker decided to drive me to Madera to see Judge Hammerberg.

On the ride down, she said she had recently become a social worker and had never met the judge. I told her I didn't like him because he was phony and rude. I'm sure she was skeptical of the opinion of an eighteen-year-old girl who had been kicked out of a foster home and boarding house within three months.

In the judge's chambers, the social worker sat next to me at the large dark mahogany oval table. I watched her restrained expression change to "what the hell" as he spewed condescending remarks.

When finished, he opened the door with a fake smile and pretentious demeanor, as if putting on a show for the employees. "Thank you for coming Kathi. Feel free to visit any time." I glared at him and thought *are you kidding me? You're acting like a nice guy after the way you just belittled me?* But as the good compliant girl, I didn't say a word.

Outside the courthouse, the social worker said, "You were right about him."

"I tried to tell you," I responded smugly. "And maybe the shrink was right about me getting my own way. I am moving back to Aunt Glo's."

Chapter 18

SOMETIMES SEX, DRUGS, AND ROCK AND ROLL LEAD TO JESUS

I returned to the Bay Area during some of the most eventful, revolutionary, and culturally defining years in history. Social and political unrest ran rampant and spanned all sectors of society. Peace activists and leftist intellectuals on college campuses protested the Vietnam War. The Black Panthers protested police brutality. Native Americans seized Alcatraz Island. Acid-dropping, pot-smoking free spirits dressed in psychedelic garb preaching "make love, not war" filled Haight-Ashbury in San Francisco.

A month after moving back to my aunt's, Neil Armstrong landed on the moon, declaring, "That's one small step for man, one giant leap for mankind." Little did I know that statement would also apply to me.

To relocate from the conservative Central Valley to the Bay Area—swarming with activists, drugs, and sexual freedom—influenced every facet of my life.

Activism aside, the effervescent Bay Area's joie de vivre fit the bill for someone primed and ready for an adventure. As did the intellectual pursuits of my dad's side of the family in abstract art, photography, and film making.

Growing up repressed in my family of twelve and inconsequential living in the foster homes, for the first time in my life, I felt valued, heard, and inspired. I had a good rapport with Aunt Glo and my cousin. I was the taxi driver for my grandmother. They had an extra bedroom so nobody had to share. Although never discussed, I believe that one Morris orphan assimilated with their lifestyle much better than ten.

Some of the most action-packed, fun-filled days of my life were while living with Aunt Glo. I couldn't wait for our weekend getaways to San Francisco, especially Fisherman's Wharf. The mecca for tourists, shopping, and eating, offered sensory overload. Cauldrons lined the sidewalk and filled the misty ocean air with the aroma of steaming Dungeness crab. The crab's bright orange shells filled the sidewalk stands alongside shrimp cocktail and seafood sandwiches. My favorite was the delectable clam chowder served in warm sourdough bread bowls.

The street performers were entertaining, as were the gift shops with tacky t-shirts and kitschy souvenirs. On the short jaunt to Ghirardelli Square, we watched the cable cars clanging along the street rails with people hanging off the sides.

I saw my first play, *Hair*, at the Geary Theater—a storied historical venue with an ornate ceiling and intimate feel. The American tribal rock musical was symbolic of the times. It had a strong anti-war sentiment mixed with the glorification of mind-expanding drugs and sexual freedom. Although shocked to see the nude scene at the end of Act One, when the actors belted out Aquarius, my purist upbringing began to dissolve.

We spent a day at Golden Gate Park exploring the de Young Museum, California Academy of Sciences, and tranquil Japanese Tea Gardens. I saw my first professional baseball game at Candlestick Park, and afterward, dined at an upscale restaurant where I savored stuffed sturgeon.

One of my favorite excursions was the ferry ride from the city to Sausalito, a picturesque seaside village with verdant hills rising from the bay and a spectacular show of magenta bougainvillea covering the quaint boutiques.

Aunt Glo's sisters also lived in the Bay Area. Each of them owned recreational vehicles—a houseboat, cabin cruiser, and motorhome. We made good use of them all, cruising the Delta and camping near Lake Tahoe. We also rented a houseboat for a week at Lake Shasta where I explored the caves and got the best tan of my life.

That summer, a year after my parent's death, a $2,500 life insurance policy surfaced, with me as the sole beneficiary. I was thrilled when my family agreed to use the money to buy me a car for college. Liberated ecstasy is the best way to describe how I felt when I drove my fully paid, maroon, 1965 Chevy Impala off the car lot.

At eighteen, with a set of wheels and a new lease on life, nothing could stop me. My friend Lee—the girl from Pleasant Hill High School—and I picked up right where we left off when the ten of us lived with Aunt Glo.

We spent nearly every weekend listening to concerts at Fillmore West and Winterland in San Francisco. Their shows were unequaled with headliners like The Grateful Dead, Iron Butterfly, and Steve Miller Blues Band. All the bands played two sets, and the music lasted until 2:00 a.m. Hippies sat on the floor smoking pot while psychedelic patterns in neon colors played on the wall behind the groups.

Stoned out of our minds by the time we left, our mandatory stop to satisfy our ravenous munchies was IHOP in Berkeley. Our uncontrollable laughter drew the attention of everyone in the restaurant. We thought it hysterical that no matter how many times we went, we were too high to decide on the type of pancake we wanted.

We explored enchanting Tilden Park, with its fragrant eucalyptus trees and grassy meadows. We sat around a campfire singing songs and turned over empty trash cans to use as bongos. Or we'd rummage through antique stores in quirky Port Costa. For years I toted around my treasured find in one of their massive warehouses—a stool made from a tan leather saddle.

Another pastime, picking up hitchhikers and one-night stands, was easy to do with the sexual revolution in full swing. Natural flirts with long hair, short skirts, and boots, we looked at the world through rose-colored glasses with one foot out of reality. Life was different in 1969. Harmless hitchhikers were everywhere, and many of them were good-looking and fun.

In September, we both settled down with classes at Diablo Valley College. I listed Liberal Arts as my major because I had no end goal. Although psychology interested me before my parents died, I decided against it, concerned I would get despondent listening to depressed people every day. The college staff assured me that deciding on a profession could wait. The challenge was direction and dedication. I soon found out I had neither.

Throughout my life, I rarely missed school. Our parents didn't allow it unless we were on our death bed. I didn't get sick. I was never late for class. I maintained above-average grades but had to work for them. Unlike some who can sit in class and absorb information from lectures, I had to take copious notes, pour over my books, and cram for tests till the wee hours of the morning.

In college, I missed classes because I couldn't wake up in the mornings. I had difficulty concentrating. Studying was a struggle. I thought I was living my best life when, in fact, I was suffering from depression. I just didn't realize it.

↤

It's been said if you can remember the 1960s, you weren't there. Truer words were never spoken for the twenty-four hours we spent at a free concert in December 1969. Lee and I, along with hundreds of thousands of other kids, left late Friday night and drove forty miles east to Livermore. The Rolling Stones and many other bands—Santana, Jefferson Airplane, and the Grateful Dead—hoped to rival Woodstock. The venue, Altamont Raceway, sat in the middle of nowhere.

By the time we arrived, the line of cars parked on the side of Highway 580 stretched for miles. We parked on the shoulder, wrapped ourselves in shawls and blankets, and walked until we saw a clearing and a drop in the terrain. As we made our way to the grandstand, we passed scores of campfires with people playing guitars and tambourines. The air was thick with camaraderie and cannabis.

We found our spot on a weed-infested knoll, passed joints and bottles of wine. The music started late morning or early afternoon, I'm not sure which because after staying up all night smoking and drinking, I slept through most of it. When I woke up, people perched on a hill opposite from us tossed a huge beach ball into the crowd below. For half an hour, it became the source of entertainment as everyone took turns batting the ball around.

The Rolling Stones, the last to play, had their set interrupted when a fight broke out. The band stopped playing for a few minutes while Mick Jagger yelled something into the crowd. The Hells Angels, guarding the stage, ended up killing a guy. We were oblivious to it all because we were high on a hill, flying higher than a kite.

Life was grand until spring 1970 when everything changed again—and not for the better. Lee and I were on a picnic with her family when she passed out. The following week, a trip to the doctor revealed she was pregnant. It was the worst possible news for her, her parents, and me.

Although the country was in the midst of a sexual revolution, abortions were illegal. A child out of wedlock was scandalous. Many young girls were coerced or outright forced to give their babies up for adoption to avoid bringing shame to their family.

Although Lee was not interested in marrying the father and did not want to keep the baby, I was shocked when her parents sent her away to an unwed mothers' home in San Francisco.

Without Lee, my only friend, I had nobody to hang around with. I visited her once at the unwed mothers' home, and although she seemed upbeat, I left depressed. The dark paneling on the walls added to the overall sense of caged shame. My heart broke when she showed me an empty wooden crib and said that her baby would be placed in it before she gave it up for adoption. I was surprised by her strength and acceptance when she said she wanted to see her baby before giving it away.

In the dark living room, surrounded by other girls with pregnant bellies, I struggled to make small talk. Their faces wore the look of desolation brought on by a world that viewed them as disgraceful outcasts. I cut the visit short and, on the contemplative drive home, vowed to never, ever get pregnant out of wedlock.

⌁

The second semester of college was coming to an end when I began dating an eccentric guy named Vince. He reminded me of Sonny Bono because he was short, had thick hair, and wore fur vests. An intriguing Bohemian character, Vince worked with oscilloscopes, played the dulcimer, and read poetry to me.

One night, Vince came to see me at my aunt's. We shut the louvered bi-folding door to the den and listened to Bob Dylan sing "Lay, Lady, Lay" on the stereo. After midnight, believing everyone was asleep, we started making out. He had a fetish for belly buttons and unfastened my belt. The sound of the brass buckle clinking must have been loud because, within minutes, we heard a knock on the door. Aunt Glo said, and not in a friendly way, "Kathi, I think it's time for Vince to leave."

I walked Vince to his car, and when I returned, my aunt had gone to bed. She refused to talk to me for the following three days. I never felt more alone and cried out every night to my parents and siblings. Not knowing what to do, I drove to Berkeley to ask her daughter Lucy for advice. She had none. I stayed for a week, and when I returned to my aunts, she exploded—accusing me of disrespecting her by having sex in her home. Nothing I said convinced her otherwise. I had no choice but to pack my things and move.

At nineteen, I felt disposable by everyone. In two years, I had been kicked out four times. Twice by Aunt Glo, the second foster home, and by the nuns at the boarding house.

I returned to Fresno in June 1970 and moved in with my friend Darcel from high school. She was a pretty blond from an upper-middle-class family. We worked part-time and smoked pot. We didn't like alcohol or hard drugs but discovered that we enjoyed sleeping pills known as reds. We dragged Belmont Avenue in either her Volkswagen bug or my Chevy Impala to buy them.

One night we bought reds from a group of shady characters—three brothers with a bad reputation. I thought the youngest one, Ray, was cute. From that night forward, whenever we dragged Belmont, we made a point of trying to find them. They couldn't figure out why someone like me would be attracted to any of them, let alone their youngest brother. And they couldn't figure out why a couple of girls who looked like us were buying drugs. Apparently, wholesome girls with cars were not their norm. They accused us of being narcs no matter how many times we denied it. To prove that we weren't, they insisted we take reds in front of them. Naïve and trusting, a Pollyanna with my head in the clouds, I should have taken their accusations more seriously because I soon found out how evil they were.

Late one night, two of the brothers, including Ray, stopped by my house and invited me to Sambo's for coffee. Initially, I declined because it was close to midnight and I hadn't felt well that day. They persisted, so I gave in.

We grabbed a booth and ordered coffee. "Kathi, why don't you go buy us some Marlboros?" Ray asked.

"Why don't you buy them yourself?"

"Because you're on the end. Here are fifty cents. The machine is over there." He pushed two quarters across the table.

"You know, I really don't feel good. You go."

"Quit acting like you're dying."

I wasn't in the mood for arguing, so I grabbed the quarters and crossed the restaurant to the cigarette machine. When I returned, they encouraged me to drink up. Not long after finishing the coffee, I spit out a piece of paper and immediately began to feel strange. "I'm really not feeling good. Can you take me home now?"

"We're not done yet. You're going to have to wait a minute."

"Then I'm going outside for some fresh air. Come get me when you're ready."

I walked across the parking lot and sat down on a curb. Instead of feeling better, I felt increasingly worse. And when the taillights on the passing cars began to leave red trails, I came unhinged. I sprinted into the restaurant and pleaded for them to take me to the hospital.

We piled into the car, and on the drive, it felt like the world was closing in. My vision was weirdly wavy, their voices sounded distorted, and I couldn't catch my breath. They weren't the most trustworthy bunch, so the closer we got to the hospital, the more agitated I became. *They're going to dump me in the parking lot and leave.*

"I changed my mind. Just take me home," I begged.

When they dropped me off at 1:00 a.m., I was in a full-throttle panic. I beat on the door while screaming at the top of my lungs, "Darcel! Hurry up! Open this damn door!"

After what seemed an eternity, she opened the door. "Kathi! What's going on? What the hell is wrong with you? Why are you kicking the door down?" Her face was fixed in confusion.

"I think I'm dying! You need to take me to the hospital—now!"

"What do you mean you think you're dying?"

"I don't have time for all your questions! Just take me to the hospital!"

"Okay! I have to get dressed!"

While I argued that we didn't have time for her to get dressed, she pulled her pants on and continued to question who I was with, where we went, and what we did.

As I watched her dress in slow motion, I screamed, "Why are you taking so long?"

"Kathi, I am moving as fast as I can! You are acting so weird! I think they put something in your coffee."

"Why do you think that?"

"Because I am not moving slow! I'm putting my clothes on faster than I ever have, and you are acting like you're out of your mind!"

Darcel was an intelligent girl with a good head on her shoulders. I trusted her. I took inventory of how I was feeling and decided she must be right.

"Okay, well, maybe the hospital can give me something to stop this."

"If I take you to the hospital, they'll put you in the G ward and won't let you come home for three days."

As freaked out as I was, the thought of staying locked up in a looney bin with crazy people did not appeal to me. Relieved that I wasn't dying, I resigned myself to ride it out and went into the bathroom. Darcel's diagnosis was confirmed when the bathroom door began to drip like a burning candle.

I laid down on the sofa and blacked out.

When I awoke hours later, Darcel was kneeling next to me, crying and saying the Rosary. It frightened me—I knew I must be dying for her to pray over me. I blacked out again and encountered God, who assured me I would be fine. I didn't see Him as much as I felt energy immersed in black space. I woke up and told Darcel, "You don't have to worry. I just spoke to 'The Man,' who said I'd be fine." We both laughed.

I woke up the next morning still tripping. Everything I had heard about hallucinogens was right. The music sounded better. People and furniture looked smaller or taller just by willing it. I fixated on a wilted rose, and when I told it to bloom, it fluffed and turned vibrant red. My pigtails felt like appendages growing from my head. Although that day was not as horrific as the night before, I was happy when I woke up the following day feeling like myself again.

Two weeks later, we ran into the hoodlums who drugged me. I asked what they did and why. I will never know if they genuinely put ten hits of pure paper acid in my coffee, but I understood how contemptuous they were. They haughtily explained that their goal was to take me out because they believed I was a narc intent on busting them. Their goal was to reduce me to a vegetable.

⌐

In late 1970, I began working for Kinney Shoes in the Fashion Fair Mall when a strikingly handsome Italian named Anthony walked into the store. He modeled and sold men's clothing a few shops down at Walter Smiths. He asked me out, and I readily accepted. After all the long-haired hippies and derelicts I'd been running around with, he was a breath of fresh air. Clean-cut and well-dressed, Anthony was funny, charming, and well-liked.

Our first date at the movies was surreal because nobody else was in the theater. We held hands and watched *Love Story* with Ryan O'Neal and Ali MacGraw. He visited every day and by the following weekend, we were engaged. At dinner he surprised me with a beautiful marquis cut diamond ring that he had dropped into my cocktail.

I began planning our wedding, chose my bridesmaids, and selected their dresses. He took me to his mother's house in Auberry, where we created the guest list.

In December, he wanted to buy Christmas gifts for all my siblings. We spent days at the mall where I chose meaningful gifts for each of my brothers and sisters like a butterfly ring for Theresa and a skirt for Carole. Anthony pulled out his checkbook and paid for everything. My family was thrilled Christmas Eve when we showered them with beautifully wrapped packages.

The next day, we spent Christmas at his mother's. Anthony gifted me with a sapphire and diamond heart-shaped ring and necklace. I felt like a princess, and he was my prince…until January rolled around, and I discovered his true colors.

I started catching him in lies. Some of them insignificant, like telling me he was at his aunt's when I knew he was at his friend's house. But the deal-breaker was when every one of the checks for my siblings' Christmas gifts bounced, and a jeweler knocked on my door to collect the jewelry.

I called off the engagement, and two weeks later, I discovered that I was pregnant. Anthony had already suspected it because of the changes to my body. When I told him his suspicions were right, I added that I didn't want to see him ever again. He threatened to take me to court and prove that I was an unfit mother by paying three guys to testify I had sex with them. The next time he called me, I told him I had started my period. "I'm not pregnant, so there's no reason for you to call me anymore."

"I bet you're happy."

"Yes, I am. Now leave me alone." That was the last time I spoke to him and marked the end of another chapter in my life.

For the following months, unrelenting anxiety and never-ending head chatter tormented me. *What am I going to do? No man is going to want me if I have a baby. How will I support a child?*

I did not want to be pregnant, and even though I considered abortion, I knew I could never go through with it. The commandment "thou shalt not kill" does not come with a disclaimer. My fear of burning eternally in hell because of a bad decision prevented me from seriously entertaining the thought.

My options were to keep the baby or give it up for adoption. Neither option appealed to me. I did not want to be a mother, but the thought of my child growing up without me was equally unbearable. My only hope was to miscarry. But what if I didn't?

The grueling, soul-searching, anxiety-ridden merry-go-round drove me mad. So I decided to visit Grandma Lachawicz to get her advice.

When I arrived at her house, she was busy setting the table for Grandpa's lunch. She placed the dark rye bread near his plate as she said, "Kathi, everyone thinks you should give the baby up for adoption."

"Who is everyone, Grandma?" I asked while watching her from the sofa in the living room.

"My friends."

"Your friends? Do they know me?" She knew I was annoyed and looked at me without responding.

"People who don't even know me think they know what's best for me? How does that work?" I left her house more agitated than when I had arrived.

As the months rolled on and it became apparent that I was not going to miscarry, I decided to take Grandma's advice. She had recommended an adoption agency called the Infant of Prague, so I called and scheduled an appointment. During their interview, they questioned why I wanted to relinquish my child. Satisfied with my answers, they reassured me that I made the right decision and had me sign papers.

In September 1971, I went into labor. *Hard labor.* Excruciating labor. I was in so much pain that I told them to kill me and take the baby. Eventually, they induced labor, and I had a baby girl at 2:00 a.m. As soon as I delivered, they whisked her away so I couldn't see her.

For three days, five women and I shared a hospital room. The first day the nurses brought all the women their babies, but not mine. The second day, when it happened again, I demanded to see my daughter, but they did not bring her. On the third day, I raised hell. That afternoon, the nurse placed her in my arms, and I understood why they had denied me.

My bed by the window had sunshine filtering through the blinds. The sunlight bathed her little face when she opened her perfectly shaped eyes and looked up at me. Tears fell from my cheeks onto hers. She was so tiny, only 5 lb. 6 oz., with a full head of dark hair and soft blue eyes. Overcome with emotion, I held her tight and rocked her as my mind tried to grasp reality. *She is the most beautiful little girl I've ever seen. She is my baby. There is no way that I can give her up. I am not giving her away.* I continued to cry and rock her until the nurse returned and insisted I hand her back. When I resisted, she said, "She is not your child. You signed adoption papers."

Later that day, a representative from the adoption agency arrived. When I told her I changed my mind, she replied it was too late; they had already taken my daughter to a study home. I would have to wait a week before I could pick her up. The hospital gave me a shot to dry up my milk and told me to get dressed and go home. Aimless and lost are the best words I can use to describe how it felt to be pregnant for nine months, give birth, and go home without my baby.

The following week when I went to the Infant of Prague to pick up my daughter, a woman kept me in her office for two hours, trying to coerce me to go through with the adoption. I stood my ground. When she understood I wasn't leaving without my baby, she left the room and returned with my cherished daughter. I named her Cherise.

‿

When Cherise was three months old, my sister Judy and I moved in together. It was a two-bedroom, one-bath, unfurnished apartment. And when I say unfurnished, I mean it literally. We had no furniture other than a bassinet a friend had given me. Judy and I slept on the floor. Our stereo was a transistor radio that we put on top of a glass to amplify the sound.

I was on welfare, and Judy's job paid minimum wage. We celebrated like rock stars the day we made our first purchase: a dinette from Whitefront. We finally had a place to sit while we ate meals like Hamburger Helper, the only food we could afford.

I was still living the fast life dating various men and smoking weed. On April Fool's Day, 1972, when Cherise was six months old, I smoked pot for the last time. Leading up to that day, I was growing weary of the people surrounding me who took drugs, and the fact that I was a mother running the streets was eating at me.

One night, I sat on the floor with her on my knees, looked into her innocent little face, and said, "You are my daughter. I am your mother." It didn't feel real, so I had to convince myself of the truth. *She depends on me. Mom did not drink or take drugs, so neither should I.* I quit cold turkey and never looked back. I was twenty-one years old.

A month later, I was lying on the sofa watching television when Judy stepped into the living room and asked me if I was okay. Her question triggered panic because I hadn't been feeling well. I thought by her asking the question, I must have looked sick and began to hyperventilate. Judy insisted on taking me to the hospital because neither of us had seen or heard of anyone hyperventilating.

In the emergency room, the doctor diagnosed my condition as an anxiety attack and said I had nothing to fear. I'd never heard the term and questioned how he knew it wasn't a brain tumor. After explaining the differences between the symptoms of a brain tumor and a panic attack, he sent me away with a prescription for valium. I wasn't convinced, and told him if I died, I wanted my tombstone to read, "Doctor Jimin said it was anxiety."

A few months later, Judy moved out. I was still on welfare and couldn't afford the apartment independently, so I moved in with Mom's best friend from high school, Jane, and her husband. She had nine children. The oldest was the same age as me, and her youngest the same age as my daughter. Her two oldest had married and moved out, so between her seven, Cherise, and me, it felt like I was at home again.

Jane was a practicing Catholic, non-judgmental, gracious, and soft-spoken. She didn't wear her religion on her sleeve and led by example, not by preaching. While I lived with her, we had many conversations about God, the Bible, and Catholicism. To my dismay, I discovered that after a lifetime of Catechism and church, all I learned was how to recite prayers. I certainly didn't have a relationship with Jesus and questioned everything: the existence of God, Heaven, Satan, and Hell. I was shocked to learn Jesus didn't sit down and write the Bible. And when I understood that mere mortals wrote it, I doubted its validity.

I questioned Jane about everything. All of her answers to my questions sounded mysterious or far-fetched, so I asked her, "Jane, how do you know for sure?"

"I have faith."

"What does that mean?"

"It means I believe. Pray about your questions, and God will give you the answers."

"That doesn't make sense. How is God going to answer me? Am I going to hear voices?"

"No, you will just know."

"I will just know?"

"Yes, you will just know."

And that was the end of it. Jane never got flustered, but I always left the conversations feeling frustrated.

While living with Jane, my anxiety attacks became more frequent and intense. I learned later I had agoraphobia, but at the time, didn't know my disorder had a name. I still believed I had a brain tumor or was going insane. I became attached to Jane in an unhealthy way. She became my tranquilizer and lifeline. I couldn't have her out of my sight for any length of time, or it would throw me into a panic attack. Jane, aware of how anxious I was, invited me to go to Mass with her, but I declined out of fear. The entire world was scary.

⌣

While living with Jane, I enrolled in the Electronic Computer Programming Institute (ECPI). I learned how to write computer programs for the Univac 9200 to become a systems analyst. The trade school was cutting edge. Nobody owned a computer in those days. I studied Basic Assembly Language (BAL), Common Business Oriented Language (COBOL), and Report Program Generator (RPG). I was the only girl in the first graduating class of seven. Although I was guaranteed a job after graduating, I was turned away at every company I applied for. When learning that I was a single twenty-one-year-old mother, their frequent response was for me to return to school. It was 1972, a time when women were still struggling to break through a man's world.

While enrolled at ECPI, I caught the eye of the director, Jim. He owned a Datsun 240Z sports car covered with racing decals and had a great sense of humor. When he asked me on a date—dinner at his apartment—I readily accepted. That night, while frying chicken, he explained that he was a Mormon and a bishop in his church.

We continued to date and discuss religion. One evening Jim told me he wore garments and wanted to get married in the temple. If we were to marry, I would have to join the Church of Jesus Christ of Latter-Day Saints (LDS). I was still searching for answers and badgering Jane about my Catholic faith, so when Jim asked me to consider converting, I agreed.

I met with the missionaries and read the Book of Mormon. Throughout the process, I discovered that Catholicism was very different from the beliefs of LDS. I had a lot of questions and concerns.

When I expressed them to Jim, his response was the same as Jane's, "Pray about it!"

Between my panic attacks, Jane, and Jim, I prayed harder and more consistently than I had my entire life. I pleaded with God to free me from anxiety and to direct me with religion. Every single night, to help me fall asleep, I prayed the Salve Regina:

> Hail, Holy Queen, Mother of Mercy, our life, our sweetness, and our hope. To thee do we cry, poor banished children of Eve. To thee do we send up our sighs, mourning and weeping in this valley of tears. Turn then, o most gracious advocate, thine eyes of mercy toward us, and after this, our exile, show unto us the blessed fruit of thy womb, Jesus. O clement, O loving, O sweet Virgin Mary! Pray for us, O Holy Mother of God, that we may be made worthy of the promises of Christ. Amen.

If reciting the prayer once didn't work, I prayed it a thousand times more.

The panic attacks made me feel like I was holding on by a thread. My head felt like it was in a vise. Often, I would be too dizzy to walk and have to hang onto the walls. My face and neck would get so flush and hot that I carried a cold washcloth for the back of my neck and hovered over sinks to splash cold water on my face. My stomach knotted up until I felt disoriented and unable to take a deep breath. Most unsettling was that the attacks came out of nowhere, for no reason, often several times a day. I could never relax. Not knowing what was going on, I truly believed I was going insane.

Up until that time, I never got sick or had headaches. I was a free spirit willing to do anything, anytime, anywhere. With the panic attacks, my life was reduced to a constant heart-pounding, head-exploding, anxiety-ridden neurotic trying to make it from one hour to the next. The only thing that kept me going was my daughter. I had to stay sane for her.

Until the day I cracked.

It was a sunny Saturday afternoon when I got into my car, rolled up the windows, started driving, and let out a blood-curdling scream. And then more screams. And when I couldn't scream anymore, I began crying out. "God! Help me! I'm going insane! I can't take it anymore! I need you! You are the only one that can help me! Please! Help me!" I sobbed and screamed and drove until I had nothing left. When I returned home, I told Jane I wanted to go to church with her.

On Sunday, while getting dressed to go to Mass, I felt another panic attack coming on. The last time I had been to church was at my parent's funeral four years earlier when I was an innocent virgin. Before sex, drugs, and rock and roll. I thought that as a tainted heathen, the minute I stepped into the church, the roof would come crashing down.

We parked across the street in front of St. John's, the school I attended in eighth grade with the scary nuns. When I exited the car and turned to look at the church, I became overwhelmed.

St. John's held a lifetime of memories. At my confirmation, Mom and I took a photo together in front of the life-size, stark white statue of Jesus outside the church. I went to Mass there with my grandparents during summer vacations and on Christmas Eve. When the chapel, lit solely by holy candles, felt more divine and sacred than the entire year.

WE WERE THE MORRIS ORPHANS

The baby Jesus laid in a manger at the foot of the altar while our voices rang out, "Oh, Come, Let Us Adore Him."

The familiar Gothic-Romanesque style building—made of red brick with two spires and simple crosses perched on top—suddenly felt threatening. Four years was a long time to commit mortal sins. I'd broken every commandment other than thou shalt not kill.

Jane and I crossed the street and began the climb up the stairs. As we inched closer to the triple-arched entrance, my heart beat faster. "Jane, I think I'll just wait outside." She gave me a sideways glance as if to say, "Oh no, you're not," and kept walking. I followed her inside; after all, she was my lifeline.

Although I had seen the interior many times before, that day it took my breath away. *This must be what heaven looks like.* Opulent grandeur covered every inch. From the celestial fresco adorning the concave ceiling to the massive stained-glass windows depicting the saints. As we walked up the center aisle to our seats, I stayed focused on the wall behind the altar. The fresco had a baby blue backdrop with angels resting in fluffy white clouds. God in a flowing robe, Jesus holding a cross, and the Holy Spirit depicted as a white dove.

We sat in the middle of the church on the hard wooden pews with ornate carvings on the sides. I knelt and began praying piously, begging for God's help.

As communion neared, I became more anxious. If the roof was going to cave in, that would be the time. Catholics believe the eucharist becomes the body of Christ. Jesus, present in the church, knowing I was in a state of mortal sin, would surely punish me somehow.

While the rest of the congregation filed to the altar, I remained kneeling and began to cry. *Lord, I know I am a sinner. I know I am not worthy. Please forgive me. I need you.*

At that moment, I felt a power, an indefinable energy tug at the center of my chest—like a ten-ton magnet drawing me to the altar. As the pull intensified, I became acutely aware of God's presence and forgiveness. As I sobbed with gratitude, He downloaded the answers to every single question I'd prayed about. I knew I was home. I knew I was Catholic.

I just knew.

Chapter 19

A BRIEF GLIMPSE INTO MY ADULTHOOD

Jane asked me to move out after living with her for a year. She felt that my attachment to her was unhealthy. Like a mother bird teaching her fledging to fly, she gently coaxed me out of her nest. She hoped that the detachment would help with my agoraphobia. It didn't. However, alone in the world as a single mother, I had to figure things out quick.

To provide for my daughter I applied for welfare and found out that I had too much pride to continue with the program. Unable to land a job in computer programming, I took the civil service test for the Internal Revenue Service (IRS) and was hired in early 1973. It was there that I met my husband. We married in 1977, had a son, and divorced twenty-two years later.

Five years after my divorce, at age fifty-four, I was diagnosed with ovarian cancer. The tumor was the size of a cantaloupe. I had a hysterectomy, underwent chemotherapy, and never missed a day of work during treatments. Four years later I retired from IRS with thirty-five years of employment.

My life experiences as a wife, mother, career woman, divorcée, and cancer survivor could fill several more books. For the purposes of this book, it is important to know that I married and had a son and a daughter.

Part Two

MY SIBLINGS' AND PARENTS' STORIES

~~∞⊘∞~~

Chapter 20

MY SIBLINGS AND FOSTER HOMES

Once I left the second foster home and moved into the boarding house, I was on my own. However, my nine siblings remained together for a total of three years. When removed from the third foster home, they were split up. Some were in groups of two or four, and some lived alone with family or friends.

Over fifteen years, between the ten of us, we lived in nine different foster homes with relatives, strangers, the boarding house, and the parents of friends.

Some of the homes were nurturing; others were not. Some of my siblings look back fondly at their living conditions. Most do not. We were all abused in one form or another, causing three to run away, two to spend time in juvenile hall, and three of us to have children out of wedlock.

The physical abuse usually targeted the meekest siblings: Jeff and a sister. At one house, Jeff's chores included watering the front lawn by hand. There was a spot where a dog stopped daily to urinate, which caused the grass to turn yellow—no amount of watering would help. The foster father accused Jeff of not watering the area, and when Jeff protested, he beat him with his belt. Jeff was only eight years old.

That same man abused my sister because he believed her dress was too short. After reprimanding her, he picked her up and threw her ten feet across the bedroom—her head slamming against a thick wooden headboard. She has spine issues to this day. The second time he bent her over his knee and spanked her while she was wearing a skirt. When he caught her stealing cigarettes, he took her to the basement with a two-by-four. That incident traumatized her to the point that she has no recollection of what he did to her in the dark recesses of that room.

Three of my siblings were sexually abused. Not physically, but emotionally. A foster father walked around the home naked in front of my brothers while he had an erection. His wife would hover over my brothers in her nightie while not wearing panties. Another foster father, while driving my sister home after she babysat, would pull over and try to make out with her.

In two of the foster homes, my siblings were starved. Jeff was once so hungry he ate an entire onion. The mother in a neighboring house, aware of my siblings' deprivation, secretly invited them over to feed them. It was while living in that house that my brothers began stealing.

After school the bus dropped my brothers off near an old run-down liquor store and bait shop. The owner sat in the back room and watched a small black and white television while my brothers walked through the store. They had cleverly hollowed out some old history books and challenged each other to see who could steal the most or lift the biggest prize. Once outside, the bantering for bragging rights began.

"Hey, Mike! Show me what you got!" challenged Jeff. Mike, the sweet-toothed wonder, opened his book to display his stash of bubble gum, candy, and his most prized pilfer: candy cigarettes.

Jeff, not to be outdone, walked stiff legged toward Mike and proudly exclaimed, "Yeah, well, I got you beat!" He reached down inside his jeans and pulled out a frog gig—the fork-like prong used to spear frogs.

"Ha! Ha! You're kidding me!" Mike was clearly impressed.

"If you think that's bad, wait till you see this!" Jeff opened the cover of his book to reveal a bag of snuff! Little did he know his treasure would lead to another beating.

The foster father found the snuff tucked in a pocket of his jeans. One of my sisters, ironing near a window, witnessed the foster father drag Jeff to the back yard, grab a fence slat, and beat him as he held him with one arm. He left red welts with every strike to Jeff's back and legs. My sister was reluctant to report the beating because when placed in that foster home, the probation officer warned them, "If we have to move you one more time, we'll send you to an orphanage!"

One of the homes was run like a concentration camp. My siblings had their food rationed, ate in shifts, and were sent to bed by 7:00 p.m. My brothers lost weight in that foster home. They were always hungry and looked forward to unsupervised mornings when they could eat their fill of skim milk and cheap industrial cornflakes. At night, they snuck saltine crackers, and when caught, they were punished for stealing food.

They were also treated like laborers and housekeepers. The older girls spent weeks scraping the paint off a staircase and windowpanes with razor blades. When completed, they were ordered to paint not only the windowpanes and stairs but the hallway and basement.

My sisters cleaned the house while the foster mother sat every night with a cocktail. She used her finger to run across places too high for the girls to reach, and yelled at them if she found any dust. She was condescending, called them names and made them feel inferior with remarks like, "I don't know how you made pep girl with you being so fat!"

My teenage sisters, all in high school and of varied proportions, begged for bras. The foster mother bought padded pointy pink bras from the grocery store, all in the same size. It was incredibly embarrassing—not only because none of the bras fit properly, but because they were visible through the white blouses of the girl's school uniforms.

One foster father would barge into the bedroom while my sisters were dressing, so the girls began changing in the closet.

My sister Linda asked to go to the prom and was told by the foster mother that she would have to make her own dress. Linda sewed her gown during her sewing class at school. When she asked for money to get her hair done, the foster mother refused and told her to use the money she earned by babysitting. She also refused to buy a boutonniere for her date because he was Hispanic. Heartbroken for my sister, my sister Judy picked roses and ferns from their yard and created one for him.

The night of the prom, the foster mother took pictures of Linda and her date as they smiled and posed for the camera. When they left the house, the foster mother removed the film from the camera and threw it into the roaring fire in the fireplace as my siblings watched in horror.

That same foster home took a family vacation to San Francisco with their son and sent my siblings to summer camp. For my sisters, it was more like boot camp. They had to backpack twenty-two miles through elevations ranging eight thousand to ten thousand feet, with none of the essential equipment like hiking boots or sleeping bags. The foster home sent them with lightweight sleep sacks that kids use for home sleepovers. With nighttime temperatures dropping into the thirties, my sisters huddled together in the same sack, used the other to cover themselves, and still froze to death.

The foster family returned from their vacation refreshed with new suits and dress ensembles. Their son returned with a minibike. The Morris kids returned exhausted and with blistered feet.

Between social security benefits and the trust fund, there was no basis for my siblings to go hungry or without... so why did they? Could it be that the social security payments intended to feed and clothe my siblings were misused? My sisters became suspicious of misappropriation when one home had bars installed on the outside of the windows. They also had the exterior of their house stuccoed and painted.

Foster parents bought new furniture to fill an empty living room, installed wall-to-wall carpeting and reupholstered Louis XIV furniture. They also converted their garage and remodeled the dining room.

My siblings alerted visiting probation officers to the home improvements, hunger, and abuse, yet no actions were taken.

Although I knew about the abuse, I felt there was nothing I could do. I was branded the black sheep because I lived in the Bay Area and smoked pot. However, everything changed the day Grandma Morris asked to visit her grandchildren. The foster mother agreed she could see them, but not at her home. Grandma had to see her grandchildren—her flesh and blood—in the basement of a local business.

Disrespecting our grandmother infuriated me. I went to the Madera courthouse and demanded to see the judge. I made it clear that I would report them and expose the abusive foster home to the news media if my siblings were not removed. It was the first time I felt empowered because of the notoriety. My siblings were removed that same week.

Most of the foster homes did not provide the basic needs or fundamental craving of orphans—a loving, nurturing environment. Some resumes checked off all the boxes: a Catholic family in a large house that attended church and sent us to Catholic schools, but nothing more.

The media attention and the worldwide outpouring of money and offers to keep the ten Morris orphans together failed. Each of us was forced down different paths. Some more intense than others. Some more perilous than others.

Like Michael.

Chapter 21

MICHAEL ANTHONY

Michael, the eighth child and the second boy, was born in 1958 in Orange, California, on Grandpa Lachawicz's birthday. Their shared birthday built an early connection between the two of them. When Grandpa visited, he never failed to bring a special treat, usually graham crackers, just for Mike. The twinkle in Grandpa's eye and the smile on Mike's face kept the rest of us from getting jealous. We understood and accepted their bond.

Mike, full of spunk and personality, was a handful and a manipulator. When he was two, Mike threw the first of many tantrums where he held his breath until he turned blue. Our parents and grandparents panicked. We girls instinctively knew he would be fine and laughed at the sight of him changing colors. We received a reprimand, and Mike got the attention he craved. As he grew older, holding his breath fell to the wayside. He found other ways to stay center stage.

Mike had a mind of his own and excelled academically. Short and cute with blue eyes and thick sandy blond hair combed like a surfer, the girls in grade school viewed him like a little doll and fought to carry him around. The attention helped shape his confidence and cockiness.

Mike was ten years old when our parents were killed. All my siblings were together for the first three foster homes. After the third foster home, they were split up. The four boys: Robert, Mike, Jeff, and Ed, were placed with our grandparents when Mike was thirteen.

Initially, life was good living with our grandparents. My brothers knew them best, and there was no abuse or hunger. Their only complaint was that our grandparents were disciplinarians approaching their seventies and lived a quiet life.

Mike was resourceful and always had money. He worked odd jobs and babysat the neighborhood kids. One year, eager to go to summer camp with his school, our grandparents told him he would have to earn his way. He built a wagon and loaded it with boxes of peanuts. Every weekend for a month, he walked ten miles and solicited from offices and homes until he collected the amount he needed.

He attended San Joaquin Memorial High School (SJM), which was within walking distance of our grandparent's home. His freshman year, he was still short at 4'10" with an athletic build and enough moxie to try out for the basketball team. He made the team and would boast, "I might be short, but I'm quick and fast!" He also played flag football and was on the swim team for two years. By the time he began his senior year, he had grown a foot and stood 5'10".

Our grandfather liked to bet on horseraces. He taught Michael how to handicap and took him to the racetrack at the Fresno Fair. I tagged along once. Grandpa didn't sit down and worked the race form like a job. He told me who to bet on, and when he didn't have a clue, he laughed and said, "Just pick your favorite color." Mike, who adored our grandfather, soon followed in his footsteps with an affinity for gambling. Not only at the tracks and playing cards, but with life.

Mike's high school senior year had just begun when he told Robert he wanted to move out of our grandparents' home. He had no basis other than the constraints of living with senior citizens in a sedate disciplined environment. It just so happened that Robert, a few months earlier, had told their probation officer that he too wanted to move out. The probation officer said that without a valid reason, they would not remove him. His only recourse would be to run away.

Robert repeated to Michael what the probation officer told him, "She is not going to move you for no reason. You have to run away. I'll help you. Go to the school and hide in the dugout. Tonight, I'll bring you some blankets. Then tomorrow, take the bus downtown and get on a greyhound bus to L.A." So, he did.

Mike stayed in Los Angles for a week and had the time of his life. Somehow he managed to check into hotels and called Robert each time he moved. He went to his first professional baseball game at Dodger Stadium and spent a day at Disneyland. Smart enough to save for a bus ticket home, when his money ran out, he returned to Fresno. However, contrary to the probation officer's conjecture, Mike landed back at our grandparents, back at SJM, and not on the right side of anyone.

The following month Mike went to a high school football game between SJM and Fresno High School. Mike and his friends were in a car, leaving the game, when a group of guys from Fresno High approached them, talking trash about SJM losing the game. One of the boys reached through the car window and grabbed Michael. Mike stabbed him in the arm with a pocketknife. The driver sped off and dropped Michael miles away so he could walk home undetected. Later that night, Mike snuck out of the house and buried the knife in a field.

It took weeks for the authorities to determine that Michael was the perpetrator. The victim identified him by looking through yearbooks. Mike was handcuffed, arrested in class, taken to juvenile hall, and charged with attempted murder. When he went to court, the judge gave him two choices: juvenile hall or the military. He chose the latter, and, in December 1975, when he was seventeen years old, Mike joined the Air Force.

After the arrest, our grandfather believed Mike was a disgrace and embarrassment to the family and never spoke to him again. The sense of abandonment after the loss of our parents was something all ten of us felt. Our connection to our grandparents helped ground us. Because of their shared birthday and activities—like horseracing— Michael's relationship with Grandpa ran deeper than ours. Mike never recovered from the wound caused by Grandpa's alienation.

Mike was bitter that he was forced into the service, and we were sad to see him go. Stationed in Texas with no adult to support or believe in him, he knew he had to make the best of it. The first letter I received from him bragged that he was the only one in his platoon who didn't receive a demerit during locker inspections. It didn't surprise me. Michael was a force to be reckoned with.

In December 1976, exactly one year after Mike enlisted, Grandpa had a stroke. He died while watching his favorite comedian on television: Red Skelton. Grandpa's greatest fear was to die in his sleep. To protect himself, he hung a simple wooden crucifix on the wall above his bed and prayed that God did not take him while sleeping. For him to die while laughing advanced my belief in the power of prayer.

Nobody knew if Mike would attend Grandpa's funeral. Although he arrived late, we let out a sigh of relief when he showed up. He stood alone at the back of the chapel and didn't make eye contact with any of us. When the ceremony ended, he waited until most people left before he walked up the center aisle to the coffin. He took one glance at Grandpa and broke down. Seconds later, he spun around and sprinted down the side aisle sobbing, his body shaking.

Mike returned to Texas and completed his two years in the Air Force as a squad leader and aircraft dispatcher. Although he performed well, he was alone. Nobody visited him, and he did not use his R&R to come to California. His marriage to a bohemian girl with a seven-year-old son within a few months of meeting her was a desperate move spawned by loneliness.

In 1977 Mike received an honorable discharge. In early 1978, Jeff rented a U-Haul and drove to Texas to move Mike, his wife, and stepson to California. The day they arrived was electric with anticipation. We sisters hadn't seen Mike since the funeral and had never met his wife. Although we were all smiling with happiness, Mike's and Jeff's smiles were different. Their Cheshire-cat grins were a dead giveaway that they were up to no good.

As the guys unloaded the truck, their laughter grew, and we girls became more baffled. Our confusion was allayed when they removed the last of the boxes. In the back of the truck sat a vintage car. Mechanically unfit to make the long drive, my two brothers, in their infinite wisdom, built a ramp, pushed the car to the back of the U-Haul, and loaded the boxes and furniture around it. They drove sixteen hundred miles from Texas to Fresno with that load. Our chastising did nothing to diminish their strut. They were proud peacocks, and we girls, as always, were entertained.

Mike and I sat on the sidewalk, laughing and reminiscing for hours. I was so happy he was back. I teased him about his Texas accent—it just didn't fit him. It didn't take long before he lost the drawl...and the wife. I think she knew the marriage was out of desperation. She moved back to Texas, and he moved on with life.

I loved Mike's company because he gave me his full attention—like he had all the time in the world to spend with just me. I called him simply to hear him say hello with his deep, smiling, baritone voice. Speaking of smiles, when Mike smiled, it was all the way from his feet.

Hands down, he gave the best hugs ever. You knew you had been hugged and loved after a Michael hug. It was as if he squeezed all the life out of you to absorb it into himself. Sometimes it was a little too hard, where it felt like he would break your ribs. Nobody before, and nobody since, has hugged me the way Mike did.

Our brothers were full of life and shenanigans, and Mike was no exception. One summer, as Robert drove Mike through the backcountry, Mike told Robert to pull over.

"Why?" Robert asked.

"Because I know the rancher who owns this land," Mike responded with a sly grin.

Robert, who was not easily fooled, said, "No, you don't!"

"Yes, I do, and I can prove it! Farmer John told me he named all those cows after you. Now pull over, and I'll show you!"

Robert parked on the dirt shoulder. Mike got out, walked over to the wooden fence, and yelled at the top of his lungs, "Hey Robert!" Every cow turned and looked at them. Mike turned back toward Robert, winked, and said, "Told ya!"

When our sister Judy was in the hospital with pneumonia, Mike made a surprise midnight visit with his pockets stuffed with beer.

They managed to down a cold one before a nurse caught them and kicked him out. The prank lifted Judy's spirits and gave the brothers another story to one up.

Despite his good qualities, Mike's immaturity pushed people away. He could be stubborn, sarcastic, and temperamental. His pet peeve was stupid people, and for Michael, that included just about everyone.

As much as our family loved playing games, nobody liked playing with Michael. He was competitive and made our lives miserable if he lost. The card game Spades, a family favorite, was not as enjoyable to play with him. He had a photographic memory, could count cards, and had no qualms telling the other players how they screwed up.

Michael loved music. Although his favorite artist was Kenny G, one of his favorite songs was "The Greatest Love of All" by George Benson. I believe it was because the lyrics spoke to him. At every family gathering, he blasted the music so loud that nobody could hold a conversation. Woe to the person who dared to turn down the volume—Michael's wrath soon followed.

In many ways, it felt like Mike had never left, and we felt complete with him back in the fold. In many other ways, we sensed that he returned from Texas with a dark side.

Chapter 22

RUSSIAN ROULETTE

Mike was twenty years old when he returned from the service and his wife returned to Texas. On a downward spiral for the following ten years, he became an addict, drifter, and womanizer. He never held a steady job. His one attempt to establish a career was when he enrolled in a trade school for air conditioning. Brilliant, he helped teach the class but didn't complete the course. He lived with and sponged off family, and when he exhausted living with his brothers and sisters, he moved in with his girlfriends.

Sometimes he was vile. One night when he didn't like the dinner a girlfriend cooked for him, he took his arm and swept the plates of spaghetti onto the floor. He never showed remorse or apologized to the people he hurt. The further he slipped down his self-destructive path, the more bodies laid in his wake. As his circle of supporters dwindled, those of us that remained heard him repeatedly say he wanted to be with Mom and Dad.

In the late 1980s, as Mike approached thirty, his mantra for pre-
ferring death over life began to materialize. He bought a motorcycle
and rode it with reckless abandon. He lost control of his bike, hit his
head on a curb, and was found unconscious, bleeding from both ears.
He was not expected to live and spent weeks in the hospital tied to the
bed because he was combative.

When released, the doctors said Mike had made a full recovery, but Mike didn't believe it. He told us he didn't feel the same.
He thought he had damaged his brain because he wasn't as sharp as
before the accident. It bothered him immensely, so, to make light of it,
he'd laugh and say he had "drain bamage."

I believed the motorcycle accident was an attempt at ending his
life, but I had no proof. The hard evidence surfaced when he lived
with a girlfriend—the same woman whose spaghetti dinner he had
thrown on the floor. One morning he called her at work and said, "I
just called to tell you goodbye." She assumed it was because of their
fighting. When she asked where he was going, he responded with,
"Just make sure you check the garage when you get home."

She rushed home to find the car running, and a hose attached
from the exhaust pipe to the interior. He was barely conscious in the
front seat. When I got word the next day, I panicked and rushed to
their house to check on him. He looked despondent and didn't seem
happy to see me. I told him how much I loved him and how all of
us would be crushed if he had been found dead. When I asked him
why he did it, he said that he felt like a failure. No matter what he did,
he couldn't succeed. I shared with him tools I had learned in management classes with short- and long-term goals. He seemed more
annoyed than encouraged by our discussion. I left with flashbacks of
him holding his breath and turning blue when he was two years old.

Later that year, he made another attempt at taking his life. He slashed his wrists with a dull dinner knife and then called Aunt Mary. Thankfully the cuts were not deep enough to warrant a trip to the hospital. We loved him, wanted to help him, and tried to rescue him, but he rejected our every effort.

A few months later, to everyone's astonishment, he checked himself into the VA hospital for drug and alcohol abuse. He was proud of his decision to seek help. We were happy he took a step toward recovery.

Mike was in a lot of therapy during his stay at the hospital. He never missed an AA meeting. I accompanied him as much as I could. One day when I arrived, he seemed more animated than usual and eager to talk.

We were walking down a flight of stairs to the meeting when he said, "The shrink told me some great news today!"

"Really? What did he tell you?"

"He told me I never matured beyond the age of ten."

"What does that mean?"

"That's how old I was when Mom and Dad were killed. The psychiatrist said that my emotional state never matured beyond that age because of the trauma."

Mike found solace in that diagnosis because it provided him with a valid reason for his madness and addictions.

Carole, Jeff, my kids, and I went for weekly visits with plenty of candy in tow because Mike's withdrawal from alcohol made him crave sugar. We played cards, laughed, and visited as if we were at someone's home and not a hospital. We all told him how proud we were; we believed in him and would support him every step of the way.

When Mike was released from the VA to a halfway house on Valentine Street, I picked him up several times a week for a change of scenery. We went for long rides, to the movies, or to my house. I was married then with two kids. He had dinner with us, we'd play games, and then he would fall asleep. I know the sounds and routines of family life were comforting to him.

Mike stayed clean and sober and bragged each time he earned a monthly sobriety pin. When I told him how proud I was of him, he said, "Yes, but I cannot fail." I never asked him what he meant by that, and later regretted that I didn't question his response.

In early 1989, Michael left the halfway house. For his birthday in May, a group of us siblings and our families rented a cabin for a weekend at Bass Lake. We had a blast celebrating Mike's birthday and breaking in our new boat…but we were mortified that he broke his sobriety.

After that weekend, he reverted to his destructive ways times ten. In fact, he upped the ante. On more than one occasion, when he played poker with our brother Jeff and his buddies, he left the room and returned with a gun. He showed the guys one bullet, placed it in the chamber, spun it, and put the gun to his head.

A gambler fighting his demons has no business playing Russian Roulette.

Chapter 23

YES, WE BELIEVE YOU. WE ALWAYS BELIEVED IN YOU

Mike began to distance himself from the entire family after his birthday at Bass Lake. He avoided family gatherings and cut off communication with many of us for the remainder of that year and into the next. When I heard he had given away his stereo, I knew things had taken a turn for the worse. Michael lived for music.

In 1990, most of us lived in Fresno and gathered together for Thanksgiving. Although Mike didn't show up, we made the most of it and had a good time. We were a fun-loving group who played music, danced, and competed in games—such as horseshoes or billiards—regardless of who came or who didn't.

The Sunday following Thanksgiving, my sister Carole and I, along with our families, spent the day at the park enjoying the pleasant November weather. We feasted on Thanksgiving leftovers, played softball, and threw frisbees. We left the park early evening, content and happy. It had been an easy, fun-filled, laid-back kind of day.

When I returned home, the answering machine showed I had fifteen messages. *What is going on? I never have this many calls.* Aunt Mary, Uncle Dick, my sister Judy, and brother Jeff called multiple times. I listened to each recording. Every one of them said nothing more than, "Call me when you get this message." I felt sick to my stomach. *I know this is bad news. Who do I want to hear it from?* I believed of everyone who left messages, Jeff would be the most considerate when delivering the news. I took a deep breath and dialed his number.

"Hi Jeff, it's Kathi. I just got home. I was at the park all day with Carole. I've got fifteen messages from you, Judy, Dick, and Mary, so I know this isn't going to be good."

He cleared his throat, and when he spoke, I could tell he'd been crying. "I'm sorry, Kathi. We agreed we wouldn't beat around the bush with news like this. Mike's dead."

Stunned, I asked, "What happened?"

He could barely choke out the words, "He shot himself."

"Did it happen today?"

"Yes, this afternoon, about 1:00."

"It doesn't surprise me... I've been waiting for this. Where was he?"

"At Donna's." Donna was his girlfriend, who he had been living with for two months.

"Did he leave a suicide note?"

"I don't know. I don't have a lot of information. Donna called Aunt Mary because she couldn't get ahold of Carole. Aunt Mary called me. I've been trying to get ahold of you and Carole all day."

"Let's all meet at Aunt Mary's. Call Carole and tell her to meet us there."

I hung up with Jeff and was taken aback by my reaction. I didn't get emotional because I was enraged. Instead of crying, I wrestled with my anger.

Aunt Mary's ranch-style house sat on two acres in the Clovis countryside. The half-hour drive gave me plenty of time to think. *How could he? After all the times I was there for him? Every single one of us tried to help him! How could he be so damn selfish? He wasn't the only one who lost Mom and Dad. We all hurt. And he does this? So we can hurt some more?*

During my rant, a song we sang as kids intruded my thoughts: *Ninety-nine bottles of beer on the wall, ninety-nine bottles of beer, take one down and pass it around, ninety-eight bottles of beer on the wall.* The song repeated itself the entire distance to Aunt Mary's. *What the hell does that mean?*

At Aunt Mary's, we all cried, hugged, and compared notes. None of us had seen Michael in months. We didn't have any more information than Mike shot himself at Donna's that afternoon, so Carole and I agreed to go to her apartment. Jeff didn't want to go. When I turned to leave, I said, "The weirdest thing happened on my way here. The song 'ninety-nine bottles of beer on the wall' kept playing in my head. Isn't that crazy?"

Jeff's face paled, and his eyes widened. "No way! You have got to be kidding me! It played in my head too!"

Jeff and I locked eyes. It was an omen. Our entire family was going to drop like flies—one at a time. Neither of us said it out loud, but I knew we had the same thought.

Donna lived in a two-story apartment complex near Fresno State College. The fifteen-minute drive filled me with anxiety. *What will we see? What will Donna tell us?*

Carole and I parked our cars and walked together to Donna's apartment. It didn't help that Donna looked ghostlike when she answered the door. A petite brunette, all color had drained from her face, her eyes looked vacant. It was apparent she was in shock because she was barely coherent. We stepped inside, where it was unnervingly quiet. Her three kids, a ten-year-old son, a fourteen-year-old daughter, and an eighteen-year-old son, Steve, were curled together on the sofa. We hugged and cried with Donna, then asked her to tell us everything.

"Mike was mad all week. I don't know why. Every single night, he sat cross-legged on the living room floor and talked crazy shit about killing himself. He lined bullets in a row and spun the gun between his legs. He was pissing me off because he did it in front of my kids while they watched television. I told him to knock it off, and he said, 'I'm not kidding Donna, I'm going to do it.' After a week of his bullshit, last night, I yelled, 'Then just do it!'"

Donna looked at us for a reaction. I think she thought we would be angry with her. Her face relaxed when we hugged her and told her it was okay. Mike had been on a fast track to self-destruction for a long time. We felt nothing but compassion for her.

She continued, "Today, he woke up more pissed off than ever. He stomped around the house, put on his Raiders jacket, grabbed his gym bag, and left. He was gone for about fifteen minutes. When he came back, he didn't say a word. The kids went out the front door, and I went into the bathroom to get away from him. I was washing my hands when I heard the loudest boom in my entire life. It was so damn loud that it sounded like a cannon went off. I ran out of the bathroom, looked around the house, and didn't see anything. I opened the patio door and looked in the backyard. I didn't see anything out there either. About that time, Steve ran in and pushed me back into the house."

The mind sometimes does miraculous things to protect people in traumatic situations. Donna said she did not see anything in the backyard. Mike was sitting on the ground with his back against the fence. He shot himself in the forehead with a Smith and Wesson .357 Magnum, so brain matter had sprayed everywhere. How could anyone process a visual like that? Especially when it involved someone you loved?

We asked Donna to show us where Mike was sitting. It was around 10:00 at night and dark. She turned on the single dim light to the patio and led us to the fence on the northside of the yard, stopped and pointed to a spot nearest the apartment. She told us that Steve cleaned and hosed down the fence and ground after the police and coroner left. We didn't see any of Michael's remains, although as repulsive as it sounds, we tried.

The three of us stood holding hands, crying, and talking to Mike. We told him how much we loved him, then prayed The Lord's Prayer and told him to go to the light. I left close to midnight, but Carole spent the night.

The following weeks were an emotional rollercoaster when we received the toxicology and police reports. The toxicology report showed Mike tested negative for alcohol and drugs. The finding comforted the family to know he wasn't out of his mind when he killed himself. But the truth is, he hadn't been in his right mind for a very long time, so it did not comfort me. Mike suffered for twenty-two years with abandonment issues, addiction, and depression.

The police report showed that he lost against his game of Russian Roulette. There was one spent casing in the gun chamber and four more bullets in his pocket. The gun was in his left hand. He was right-handed. Was he hoping that by using his left hand, he would be unable to pull the trigger? He did not leave a suicide note; however, Donna later found a crumpled-up piece of paper on her bedroom dresser that read, *Do you believe me now?*

Mike's suicide traumatized many people, including five witnesses who either heard the blast or saw my brother. Most troubling was the information provided by two boys aged five and eight. A cyclone fence separated their backyard from Donna's. They were playing in their backyard when Mike pulled the trigger and saw everything. Their accounting was so graphic that it was redacted from the police report to protect us from the disturbing details. Mike ended his life because he never recovered from the trauma of losing his parents at the young age of ten. It angered me that he transferred his torment to those young boys to perpetuate the cycle.

↵

Michael Anthony Morris was buried on November 28, 1990, on a bitter wet, cold, foggy day. A boombox at the foot of his grey casket played songs by Kenny G. It was a simple service with a handful of friends and family. A priest gave a brief and not so meaningful eulogy as I wept uncontrollably in the front row. When the priest finished speaking, he knelt in front of me and whispered, "Kathi, why are you so distraught?"

"He shot himself so that he could go to Heaven with Mom and Dad," I sobbed. "It was all for nothing because now he is going to hell for killing himself."

"That's not true!" the Priest whispered. "We don't know what happened to Michael's soul. God is merciful. The church has softened its view on suicide and no longer teaches that people will go to hell. Only God knows the relationship Mike had with Him at the time of his death. Sadly, some people never find peace in this world."

I still struggle with it because only God and Mike know for sure.

Mike is buried at St. Peters Catholic Cemetery in the same row as Grandpa. Not next to him—at the very end. It wasn't intentional; there was no closer spot. Still, I find it achingly symbolic that in death, just as in life, Mike is alone and separated from everyone else.

⌒

It fell on us siblings to pay for Mike's burial because he had no money or insurance. We agreed to sell the gun to help pay for the expenses. The police confiscated the gun the day of his suicide, so I volunteered to follow up with the police department.

A week after the funeral, I called the police station. I explained that my brother had committed suicide, and we wanted to sell the gun to pay for his funeral. The clerk that answered the phone, a police officer, and a sergeant asked a litany of questions. They said they would do some research and call me back. When the sergeant called me the next day, I asked why he had been so hesitant. He explained that if a gun is used in a crime, they will not release it; however, because suicide is not a crime, they had no authority to retain it.

The next morning, I drove to the police department and parked in front of the junior high school located across the street. Two large grassy areas with tall pine trees lined the long walkway leading to the entrance. Although the morning was pleasant and picturesque, the thought of picking up the last thing my brother held knotted my stomach.

I entered the lobby and looked around. Chairs lined one wall. Two people were quietly completing paperwork. The room was clean, and the walls were painted pink. *Interesting. I just watched a television show where it showed how the color pink had a calming effect on inmates.*

I walked to the counter, peered through the plexiglass with a small opening at the bottom, and waited for the clerk to acknowledge me. A short woman with dark brown hair, black tailored pants, and a crisp button-down white shirt approached the window. In a stern voice, she asked, "How can I help you?"

"I'm here to pick up a gun. I called and talked to several people, including Sergeant Kravitz."

A look of skepticism washed over her face. "Who did you talk to?"

"Sergeant Kravitz," I repeated.

She lowered her head and looked over the top of her glasses. "Sergeant Kravitz said you could pick up a gun?"

"Yes. My brother Michael Morris killed himself. The police took the gun, and I'm here to pick it up. I explained this on the phone to several people already, and the Sergeant cleared it."

"I don't have any of this information. Wait right here while I check."

After a few minutes, she returned with a bald stocky officer who looked slightly more welcoming than her. The interrogation began again. Once he was satisfied with my answers, the officer handed me some forms to complete and told the clerk to get the gun.

I watched her disappear down a hall to the right. She returned with an opaque baggie and, without looking at me, placed it on the counter. She reached into the container, slowly pulled out the gun, and put it on top of the bag. I know the blood drained out of my face. Lying in front of me was the biggest gun I had ever seen, covered in blood. *Oh, my God. No. No. Is that my brother's blood? How could she be so heartless? Why didn't she warn me? She knows it was my brother.* I looked up at her, and she stared back without saying a word. I felt nauseated while my heart pounded out of my chest. It took everything in me to not burst out crying. *How can she be so cruel?*

I tried to regain my composure as my trembling hand reached into my purse and pulled out a brown paper bag. I reached through the plexiglass, grabbed the gun, and put it inside the paper bag.

"You can't do that!" she snapped.

"I can't do what?"

"You can't put the gun in that bag!"

"Why not?"

"That would make it a concealed weapon!"

"I am parked across the street in front of the school! Are you saying I have to walk to my car carrying the gun in broad daylight?"

"Unless you want to get arrested for carrying a concealed weapon, that's exactly what I'm saying!"

Outraged and eviscerated, I glared at her as I pulled the gun out of the bag and placed it back on the counter. I shoved the bag into my purse and picked up the gun. I turned, marched across the lobby, and pushed the door open with my shoulder while the gun dangled from my right hand.

Outside, there were several people headed up the long walkway toward me. *Oh my God. What are they going to think? Just keep your head down and walk faster than you've ever walked in your life.* From the corner of my eye, I could see their fear or confusion as they looked down at the gun and then up at me.

I sprinted across the walkway and street. When I reached my car, I popped the trunk, threw the gun in, and slammed the trunk door shut. My hand shook as I fumbled with the keys to open the car door. Once inside the car, my angst exploded like a volcano. I didn't recognize the bellows escaping from the depths of my soul, screaming to my brother lying in the trunk. For half an hour, I sat in my car and sobbed louder than I had at his funeral...because until that morning I hadn't seen him in a year.

And when I had exhausted all tears, Mike and I drove home— both spent, lifeless shells.

Mike's headstone, St. Peter's Catholic Cemetery, Fresno, California

Mike, 2, when he threw his first tantrum, Los Angeles

Mike, 10, Madera

Mike, 31, last photo

2-18-76
9:30 pm

Kathy and to whom it may concern,

How is ya all city-slickers. We's country folk is fucked! Yep Mike got screwed by Uncle Sam! I'm on the 2nd worst base in the whole U.S. It's dead, dead, dead here.

Theres only 100 chicks on this base! Theres 3000 dudes. Like they say,

There's no pussy
Theres no girls
So we fuck
The little squirrels.

Other than the above and whats to come I'm ok. My room-mate is cool. He's

①

from Los Angeles.

I just have to get around and maybe things will lighten up.

I start working Monday. I'm going to be dispatching pilots. I tell them what plane they are going to fly that day, and I'll do some paperwork. It'll be simple.

This base is in Del Rio. 8 miles from Mexico. At least I'll be able to go to Mexico and forget about Texas.

I'm going to take a shower now and then go to bed so I'll close this off.

②

Now don't say I didn't write to you, and you BEST WRITE BACK SOON!

Tell my niece Cherise hi and Cal too. Give Judy and Theresa my address. Ok.

Take Care

Love, Mike

P.S. I'm going to be stationed here from 1 to 2 years. Maybe I'll get out on 1 for good behavior!
HA!

Write Back its lonely here!

Letter from Mike when he joined the Air Force, Laughlin AFB, Texas, Feb. 18, 1976 (3 pages)

4-16-76
1:30 p.m.

Hi Shithead!

Just got your letter a minute ago! And you ain't gonna kick my ass! No-one is!

Your hair sure looks different, but I'm not going to make any comments! HA! HA!

I still don't know if I'm gonna make it back to Fresno or not. I might and might not! Whatever I please!

Is there any address that Robert gave you guys? If so can I have it!?

Did you trade your Pinto in for the Toyota?

Whats this shit about 36-24-36?

Oh yes mother. I haven't gotten drunk for 3 weeks. Pretty good huh!? Thats cause the last I was going to found out I'm only 17. Someone snitched!!

Maybe you do care, but those two old people could give a shit about me. The only thing they're worried about is their own conscience. I hate to even think of them because it reminds me of my old days in prison. Very depressing!

Must go so take care,

Love Mike

P.S. The other contents is for you, I hope you can use it!

Letter from Mike, Laughlin AFB, Texas, April 16, 1976 (2 pages)

Chapter 24

JEFFREY WAYNE

In late 1959, we wondered if Mom lost her mind. She was twenty-seven with eight children, including two-year-old twins, when she became pregnant for the eighth time. However, it wasn't the pregnancy that had everyone question her sanity as much as it was her obsession with the color purple. It began the afternoon she returned from the beauty salon with violet hair.

When she entered the house, our father gasped, "Joyce, what happened to your hair?"

"Nothing, Bob! I happen to like the color!" We knew to bite our tongue with her sassy response.

Unlike today where anything goes, that was a bold move. Back then, the most extreme hair colors were red and platinum blond. From there, it got progressively worse. Mom decorated and stocked the nursery with all shades of purple—the layette, baby clothes, and blankets. She never explained the genesis for her fixation, and fortunately, it vanished after the baby's birth.

Jeffrey Wayne Morris was born in June 1960 in Stockton, California. He was child number nine and the third boy. With the growing roster, he and I might as well have been a penguin and a tiger trapped together in a zoo: Kathi, nine; Judy, eight; Linda, seven; Carole, six; Theresa, four; Roberta, three; Robert, three; Mike, two; and baby Jeff.

Our nine-year age difference prevented meaningful interaction between the two of us. Our lives did not cross paths other than helping with his basic needs. It's just the way it was, and it never occurred to me it could be any different.

Jeff was the perfect baby—cuddly, quiet, and loveable with an ever-ready smile. After two years of wrestling with ornery Mike, Jeff was a breath of fresh air. However, grouped with the little kids, I saw him more as a job than someone to connect with.

Our mother ran a tight ship and expected us to help with chores. The tasks included taking care of toddlers and babies. We oldest girls had to feed, bathe, and clothe them. In that era, it was a lot of work!

Disposable diapers and premade formulas did not become mainstream until the 1970s. We used cloth diapers, safety pins, and rubber pants. Pricking ourselves with safety pins while diapering the babies hurt. Changing soiled diapers and rinsing them in the toilet was disgusting. We had a washing machine, but not a dryer. Everything had to be hung outside on a clothesline. When dry, the diapers were folded one way for boys and another way for girls. Diaper duty was a full-time job, especially with the twins.

We made the formula by mixing boiled water, evaporated milk, and Karo syrup. A dozen bottles, nipples, and caps were sterilized in big pots of boiling water, then filled and refrigerated. At feeding time, including the middle of the night, we warmed the bottles in boiling water. We tested the milk's temperature by squirting it onto our wrists. I often guessed wrong and scalded my skin. By the time Jeff rolled around, I had countless battle scars.

I couldn't wait for the baby's first birthday because it marked the end of formula and diapers. Mom's rule of thumb was when a baby turned one, they were given whole milk and began potty training. For me, that was more reason to celebrate than their birthday!

Jeff was a happy and playful toddler and grew into a shy adolescent. He had thick sandy blond hair and hazel eyes. He struggled in school to maintain average grades; however, what he lacked academically, he compensated for with his pleasant disposition.

He was nine when all my siblings were placed in the third foster home without me. He was eleven years old when placed with our grandparents, along with the rest of my brothers.

Like Mike, Jeff felt that living with our grandparents was not ideal. They were approaching seventy and did not have many extracurricular activities—a boring life for an energetic teenager.

Jeff's timid personality did not mesh well with our grandfather's thick skin. Grandpa was a product of growing up in Chicago and working in the family funeral business. His abrasive humor rubbed people the wrong way. Countless times I heard him ask strangers, "Hey, do you have a light?" If they responded with, "No, sorry, I don't smoke." His response of "I didn't ask you if you smoked, I asked you if you had a light!" was often met with a look of *you're an asshole*. Like the Godfather, you knew instinctively not to cross him.

Grandma was subservient to Grandpa. He stayed in his bedroom until noon, and when he emerged dressed in his button-down shirt, cardigan sweater, and trousers, she had a hot lunch ready for him. Grandpa believed rye bread was the silver bullet for healthy living and consumed it daily. He kept a gallon bottle of red wine close by, and Grandma kept a watchful eye over him.

Grandpa drove a taxicab for years and later became a janitor at a cleaning supply company. Not the most prestigious occupations, but he had a quiet dignity about him. He performed his jobs in a manner that commanded respect, and when he came home, he had little interaction with my brothers.

Grandma never learned to drive. She walked to the hairdresser, grocery store, and daily Mass. If the boys wanted to go anywhere, they took the bus, walked, or waited for the weekend when Grandpa might be agreeable. She had a Master's degree in music and taught piano every day in the living room. While she taught, the boys had to stay out of the house and entertain themselves. The boy's bedroom was a detached garage that Jeff shared with his nemesis, Michael. Roughhousing or all-out fighting became a way to pass the time.

In the mix was Aunt Mary, our grandparent's spoiled youngest daughter, an entitled meddling irritant. Our grandparents thought she could do no wrong, but we knew better. Although she married and moved out, Aunt Mary continued to influence our grandparents' decisions, including how to raise my brothers.

Jeff wasn't miserable, but he was unhappy and knew that without a valid reason, the court would not move him. His Godsend came while attending Sacred Heart School. He and his eighth-grade class were bussed on a field trip to Saint Anthony's Seminary in the idyllic Mediterranean real estate known as Santa Barbara. The Catholic preparatory high school sat on a hill, surrounded by lush green grass and towering trees. The trip was to encourage entering the priesthood and provide an alternative to high school.

After touring the campus, the boys listened to a pitch on the merits of living in the dorms while attending St Anthony's. As a priest intoned, "Seek God's will," Jeff's prayers were answered. With the melodic church bells cheering him on, he returned home to plead his case. He successfully convinced our grandmother of his miraculous call to a religious vocation. Before one could finish saying The Lord's Prayer, he was sent packing with their blessings. It was comical to us siblings, as we knew full well that it was a ruse to get out of our grandparents' house.

In the fall of 1974, Jeff began his freshman year of high school at St. Anthony's Seminary. It didn't take long for him to realize that he made a grave mistake. Life as a seminarian was not fun and games. It was more in line with the military. They followed a rigid schedule, each day beginning and ending in Christ the King Chapel. Every student was obligated to play all major sports. Jeff attended classes six days a week, which included Theology, Latin, and Greek. This was his schedule:

Rise	6:30 a.m.
Breakfast	7:00 a.m.
Mass	8:00 a.m.
Classes	8:30 a.m.
Supervised study	4:00 p.m.
Dinner	6:00 p.m.
Community night prayer	9:00 p.m.
Lights out	10:00 p.m.

Sundays, once a month, were reserved for secular activities like trips to the beach, movies, or visits from family. There was little room for horsing around. Still, Jeff found a way. When he jumped off a second-story balcony, he was put on notice. But when his antics included property damage, he was expelled. Jeff and a group of his friends ran full speed, headfirst, into their lockers. They left their cranial marks with perfectly formed indentations, and he earned a ticket back to Fresno in less than a year.

With Jeff's life as a devout seminarian over, our grandparents and Eddie made the trek to Santa Barbara to pick him up. Even Ed, at ten years old, had enough sense to take one look at the lockers, then Jeff, and ask why. Jeff had no answer; he only shrugged.

A lot happened while Jeff lived at the seminary. Before he left Fresno, all four of my brothers were living with my grandparents. When he returned, none of them were. Mike joined the Air Force. Robert graduated from high school and moved out. Eddie lived with Aunt Mary and her husband. Ed had been placed with Aunt Mary because our grandfather suffered a massive heart attack. When he recovered, our grandparents sold their home and moved into the Nazareth House—a Catholic senior living community.

Jeff was fifteen years old when he returned to Fresno and was placed with Aunt Mary. Both she and her husband were alcoholics, smoked like trains, and yelled constantly. Jeff and Ed lived with her for two years until one day, they returned from school and found their clothes in black plastic garbage bags at her front door. A note attached to one of them said she was kicking them out. For her to throw them out like trash was typical of her lunacy and the abuse my brothers endured living with her.

Although the way she discarded my brothers was heartless, the boys were elated that they had escaped the asylum! Jeff's last foster home was with a good and decent family. He lived with them for a year until he turned eighteen and graduated from Clovis High School in 1978.

The abuse he suffered at the hands of relatives and foster homes for ten years had ended. Whatever good there is in the world of foster homes, Jeff saw all that was evil.

Chapter 25

TICK TOCK

I was married and had two children by the time Jeff graduated from high school. For the following twelve years, we all went on with our lives.

As an adult, Jeff was the life of the party with his quick wit and humor. He stood six feet tall with movie star good looks—a rock-solid physique and megawatt smile. Charismatic, he had that special knack for bringing out the best in others. His physical attributes mixed with enviable people skills made for a chick magnet and a man's man to boot.

Jeff loved people and surrounded himself with family and friends. He was in a bowling league, hosted weekly poker games, and arranged camping trips. Not one to sit around, when we got together, we played horseshoes, billiards, or board games. One day, when he and I were shooting pool, I asked him, "If you could live your life all over again, what career would you choose?"

Without skipping a beat, he replied, "I'd become an engineer."

"An engineer? I wasn't expecting that answer! Why?"

"So I could build bridges and bring people together."

That response, and the lyrics to his favorite song, "Tick Tock" by Stevie Ray Vaughan, perfectly describe the essence of Jeff. He was a beautiful soul that drew people in.

However, he, too, had his drawbacks. Sometimes he became moody and melancholy. During those periods, he would retreat and avoid people. He drank, smoked pot, and occasionally did drugs; however, unlike Michael, he was responsible and not an addict.

Jeff lived with friends, supported himself, and was engaged for ten years. He and his fiancé's goal to save ten thousand dollars each before they married seemed impossible and the perfect excuse to never tie the knot.

Jeff worked in his fiancé's family-owned pet supply stores. He believed that when they married, they would inherit the family business; however, things changed when he suffered an accident on the job. Another employee ran into him with a forklift and gouged his ankle, which required a skin graft and a hospital stay.

When he returned to work, he felt mistreated and underpaid. The strain took a toll on his relationship with his fiancé, so he quit. He hoped a job separate from her family would provide a solid footing and move them toward marriage.

Jeff went to work for a produce company. Although he was happy to land another job, it was backbreaking work with grueling hours. He worked the graveyard shift, packing and unpacking the freezer and trucks, and drove short-haul to cities like Bakersfield. Working all night and sleeping all day took a toll on his social life. It also contributed to the demise of his relationship with his fiancé.

The years after his breakup was a dark period for Jeff. He became despondent because he felt that he wasted ten years of his life. He desperately wanted a family of his own and believed that time was running out. Looming over all of us was a sense of impending doom because so much of our family died before the age of forty. Mom was thirty-five and Dad was thirty-nine. Mom's brother, Uncle Steve, was thirty-nine when he died in a car accident five years after my parents. His son, our cousin Stevie, was thirty-six when he died in a car accident two years after Mike killed himself at the age of thirty-two.

⤳

My relationship with Jeff grew after Mike's death. It began developing when a group of us siblings met at Jeff's apartment to divide Mike's belongings. Everything Michael owned fit in a blue gym bag. Theresa took a pair of brown cowboy boots. I took his notebook, glasses, and wallet with pictures of my children. Linda took his duck t-shirts because Mike's perfect imitation of Daffy Duck made her baby son laugh hysterically.

The process had been heart-wrenching and painful. When we finished, everyone left the room except for Jeff and me. When he and I stood up to leave, he hugged me and, with a tear-drenched face, said, "I need you." I never felt as loved and valued as I did at that moment.

Later that month, Jeff and I drove in separate cars to St. Peter's Cemetery to decide on Mike's headstone. Jeff followed me in his Jeep. The halfway house on Valentine Street that Mike had lived was en route; however, I didn't realize we would have to pass it until we drew closer to the cemetery.

The closer I got, the more emotional I became. Countless times I had driven that road with the sole purpose of bringing Mike joy. I had flashbacks of him stepping out of the house, with his huge welcoming smile, and how I had tried everything in my power to encourage him and show him how much I loved him. When I reached Valentine Street, the visual of him lying in the trunk of my car—the 357 Magnum covered in his blood—threw me into a rage.

I made an abrupt right turn and came to a screeching halt in front of the two-story green weathered halfway house, bolted out of my car, and raced across the trampled lawn. I planted my feet in front of the house and screamed at the top of my lungs, "Michael! I am so pissed off at you! Why? Why did you do it? How could you do that to me? I hate you! You're an asshole! You're a fucking asshole!"

Jeff parked and ran up behind me. He wrapped his arms around my waist and held me while I choked on my sobs, screamed obscenities, and mumbled unintelligible words. He held me until I couldn't scream anymore. Bent in half, I hung over the clasp of his strong arms and hands. When I stood and turned to look at him, his eyes full of compassion, he slowly, lovingly, wiped the tears of pain from my face.

⌁

In 1991, my family moved into our custom home on four acres in Clovis. I spent a year working with the contractor on its design. Jeff was as proud of the house as I was. He often made trips during construction, carved his name on the foundation, and gifted me with a handmade mailbox that mirrored the house architecture.

I designed the house with family and friends in mind. It had a game room with a pool table and darts. A beach-entry pool, basketball court, and sunken firepit. Acreage for flag football and wetlands for frog gigging. Our house became the go-to for parties, family reunions, and holiday celebrations. So, when Jeff called me one Saturday morning in 1993, I assumed it was to plan another party.

"Hi, Kathi. How are you doing?"

"I'm good. Why are you calling me so early?"

"I have something I need to talk to you about. Is it okay if I come over right now?" His voice sounded down.

"You don't sound right. Do I need to be worried?"

"No, everything is fine. I'll explain more when I see you."

I woke my teenage son Ryan and the two of us sat in the game room waiting for Jeff to drive his forest green Jeep onto the gravel driveway. We watched through the floor-to-ceiling windows as he strolled to the door with his head down. I knew something was wrong. When I opened the door, his solemn face left no doubt. He sat on the rust-colored sofa. Ryan and I sat across from him at the glass table.

I began, "Alright, Jeff, I know something's up. If you had to come over to talk to me in person, then it can't be good."

"Only because I know you're not going to like what I'm about to tell you," Jeff murmured.

I waited anxiously for the bad news. After all the family tragedies, it was anyone's guess as to what he was going to say.

In a faint voice, he murmured, "I'm moving to Las Vegas."

My response was not as quiet. "What? When?"

"Tomorrow. I picked up a U-Haul yesterday. I'm almost done packing."

"Why? When did this happen?"

"You know I can't catch a break here. I talked to Theresa, and she said I could work for her and Jib."

"Where are you going to live?"

"She said I could live with her till I get on my feet."

"And then what? You're going to stay in Las Vegas?"

He didn't respond to my last question. What could he say? He needed to find his way in life, but I didn't want him to leave. In another universe, I would be the first to support him and say, "I want you to go and be happy." But as I died inside, all I could think was, *I want you to stay and make me happy.*

To anyone else, my reaction seemed excessive, but Jeff understood. It's why he made a special trip to tell me in person. I suffered from agoraphobia—the granddaddy of phobias—and debilitating panic attacks. It kept me housebound and limited my ability to travel, especially long distances. At one point in my life, I couldn't drive ten miles from my home without suffering a panic attack. I had made progress, but no more than one hundred fifty miles. Las Vegas was four hundred miles away! A six-hour drive from Fresno. He may as well have said he was moving to Siberia!

Jeff left and returned with the U-Haul to spend his last night with me. The heaviness throughout the house was palpable. We tried our best to mask our sadness, but the next morning was rough, especially after he and my son hugged for their final goodbye. Ryan, a sixteen-year-old teenager and a tough guy at that, began to cry. Jeff lost it, and later told me he cried the entire distance to Las Vegas.

Jeff moved in with Theresa and her husband and began working for their construction company. He was acclimating to his new normal; however, we sisters in Fresno were not doing as well. Especially Carole. She missed him terribly and made no effort to hide it. To lift her spirits, we surprised her with a plane ticket to Las Vegas for her birthday.

Carole had the time of her life. And on the night of her birthday, while partying with Jeff at Tommy Rocker's—the local's favorite bar—Jeff met the woman he had waited for all his life.

Chapter 26

THE HOLY GRAIL

Carole returned to Fresno with souvenirs and a video. My wild and fun-loving siblings videotaped their week at the Las Vegas strip, Jeff's apartment, and their crazed drunken antics. The footage included hours of entertainment, like sliding down the stairs of Theresa's house while attached together with a slinky. I called Jeff to thank him for the amusement. "Hey, dude! Whaddup?"

He responded with his coined comeback, "Not much, douchebag! Whaddup with you?"

"Carole and I are watching the videos. You guys are crazy. I'm so mad I wasn't there."

"Yeah, you missed a good time for sure. You need to get over your damn phobia!"

"Who you telling?"

"Did Carole tell you about Suzanne? The girl I met while she was here?"

"Yes, she sure did. So what's the deal?"

"We've seen each other every day. I know this sounds crazy, but I think she's the one!"

"Are you serious? You just met her!"

"I know, but she is so cool and easy to talk to."

"What does she look like?"

"She has an exotic look about her. You know how much I love Kirstie Alley. She reminds me of her. We have a lot in common. She likes the same music. She loves camping. She loves people...."

There was no containing him. He continued to gush with the enthusiasm of a kid in a candy store.

Suzanne came with a bonus: a spunky daughter named April. He adored her and called me often to brag about her wit—like the day they were waiting at a red light. When the light turned green, and the car in front didn't move, April yelled at the top of her lungs, "What shade of green are you waiting for?" He thought that was hysterical coming from the mouth of a six-year-old.

On October 9, 1993, a mere six months after meeting, Jeff and Suzanne married in a small wedding chapel in Las Vegas. He finally had everything he had been desperately seeking—a family of his own. He was young, vibrant, and handsome, with a wife and the love of his life, his daughter, April. Although Ape, his pet nickname for her, was not Jeff's biological daughter, Jeff was her father, and she was his daughter—make no mistake about that.

At thirty-three, with pent-up enthusiasm to share his life with his new family, Jeff counted down the days to take them to his favorite vacation spot: a coveted and remote place the Morris clan had frequented since 1970.

In the spectacular, thickly forested landscape of the High Sierras, meandering through a wooded valley of fragrant ponderosa pine and cedar trees runs Dinkey Creek. Nestled alongside the creek sat Jeff's holy grail—Camp Fresno.

Camp Fresno has fifty-one rustic cabins scattered among majestic pines, granite outcrops, and well-hiked trails. At the base of the camp sits a clubhouse with daily activities and a playground.

Dinkey Creek, named after a dog killed by a grizzly bear, teases anglers with brown and rainbow trout. Its gently flowing pristine water provides a playground for kids, including rocks positioned perfectly for leaping. Spanning the creek is a ninety-foot arched timber bridge. Built in 1938, it was closed to traffic in 1965. Its massive wooden trusses are the perfect backdrop for pictures or watching the creek below.

A few miles from camp are the slicks and honeymoon pool. The deep twenty-foot pool, filled with chilled water from the snow runoff, is perfect for diving. A shallow swimming area includes a rockslide covered with slippery moss. Huge sloping granite rocks invite lounging or sunning to warm up after a dip in the icy water.

The creek, swimming holes, and magnificent trees are nature at their finest. Mother Earth, coupled with the night sky illuminated by an array of glistening stars, was indeed heaven on earth for Jeff.

And so it was, in the summer of 1994, that Jeff excitedly introduced his new bride and daughter to his treasured vacation spot and the Morris clan traditions. For a week, twelve of us shared three cabins and created unsurpassed lifelong memories.

Jeff bellowed, "I love the mountains!" as soon as he stepped out of their packed, dirt-covered Jeep. My brothers belted out those four words for as long as I could remember. We all loved the mountains, but it takes a special kind of person to love the rustic cabins at Camp Fresno. They provide shelter from the elements but little more.

The bedrooms contain wire bunks with thin mattresses. Sleeping bags and plenty of blankets are a must, because at six-thousand feet, it gets chilly! A closet holds a porcelain toilet aged white to yellow. The kitchen includes a worn wooden dinette with four dilapidated chairs and a vintage white, rusted, wood-burning stove. There is no hot running water, only cold, found at the kitchen sink or outside faucet. Nor is there a tub or shower. Bathing requires a walk through soft powdered dirt to one of the outside communal shower houses. Outdoor showering is fun, but the walk back is maddening because clean feet in flip flops get frosted with a chocolate-colored film. Outside, a picnic table and fire ring complete the bare minimum necessities.

As we were busy putting things away, Jeff crept up behind me, grabbed my tit, and yelled, "Tittie twister!"

"Ow, you punk! That hurt!" I punched him as hard as I could.

He laughed, "You know you have to be on high alert now!"

Jeff was a dedicated student of *Saturday Night Live*. He repeated lines he learned from the show or created his own, using us as unwitting supporting actors. He'd shove two fingers toward our face and say, "Poke eye!" Or act like he stuck his finger up our butt, put his finger under our nose, and say, "Can you mell it?" He addressed all of us as "weirdo," "butt nugget," or "douchebag," and none of us seemed to mind. It was all in good fun and entertaining. I lovingly referred to all his little antics as Jeffisms.

Our week was jam-packed with frolic and fun. We had horseshoe and ping pong tournaments. Hiked through the cool woods, mountain meadows, chaparral, and thick brush. At the swimming hole, April, in her little girl bathing suit, showed us how fearless she was by jumping off a precarious crag into the pool twenty feet below. We had a birthday celebration where we decorated camp with streamers and balloons. We joined in the clubhouse activities with face painting and braiding colorful lanyards. Kids and adults alike scaled the huge granite outcrops surrounding our cabins for some downtime. Dinners were nightly feasts and included a fabulous fish fry generously offered up by the creek.

The most anticipated event was the men's bonfire challenges. Each night a different guy built the biggest, tallest, intense beast for nothing more than bragging rights. The better part of their day was spent foraging kindling and dry wood. At night, the designated contestant crafted his shrine while we grabbed lawn chairs and formed a circle around the fire ring. The contender fed the fire until it became a towering inferno of furiously angry flames commanding we retreat ten feet or more. Once the fire reached its highest level, we took pictures of the sculptor flexing his muscles. The following night, the contest was repeated by the next contender. Quite frankly, their competition freaked me out. The flames were so high that I feared the trees would catch fire and burn down the forest.

Once the bonfire had quieted to a reddish-orange glow, we made smores, hot chocolate, and played board games. Quiet time was 10:00 when we were expected to keep the noise to a low roar. That rule was wasted on us as we howled and laughed our asses off late into the night.

We capped our evenings with midnight walks on matted brown pine needles. Our flashlights bounced off the towering trees silhouetted against the splendor of the night sky as we made our way to Dinkey Creek Bridge—the perfect stage for late-night wrestling.

Exhausted, we retreated to our cabins, serenaded by the crackle of the dying embers and the wisps of smoke rising in upward spirals.

Mornings were divine, waking to the crisp air, devoid of all sound apart from branches snapping as Stellar jays flew from tree to tree. The morning sun breaking over the mountain and the smell of fresh coffee brewing over the campfire beckoned all to come out and play.

Dinkey Creek was food for the soul for Jeffrey.

Chapter 27

YOU ARE
MISSING FROM ME

Invigorated from our vacation, Jeff returned to Las Vegas and began
to search for a home. In the fall of 1994, I received another phone
call from Jeff where he couldn't contain his excitement. He found the
perfect house, under construction, and early enough to choose colors
and materials. Jeff had reached all his lifelong goals: a wife, his precious
daughter, and homeownership. Everything was falling into place.

That is, until a Tuesday morning, January 31, 1995. Jeff and
Suzanne were sitting at the dining room table drinking coffee when
Jeff fell to the floor, convulsing with a grand mal seizure. As he lay seiz-
ing and foaming from the mouth, Suzanne called 911. Within minutes
an ambulance arrived and rushed him to the hospital.

In the emergency room, Jeff had more seizures. The hospital
admitted him and immediately ran a battery of tests. Suzanne called

me, explained everything, and promised to keep me informed. I drove to Carole's, and together we kept vigil while waiting for Suzanne's updates. Initially, we were concerned but not overly nervous because Jeff was young, healthy, and active.

Suzanne called throughout the day and relayed details of her conversations with doctors and test results. With each passing hour and no definitive answer, our anxiety grew. Adding to our angst—we could not talk to Jeff because he was heavily sedated. Carole and I waited nervously the entire day and into the early evening.

And then we got *the* call from Suzanne.

"Hi, Kathi. We got the results of the MRI, and it doesn't look good. The scan shows large lesions in his brain near his temple and another on the top of his head. The doctor is advising immediate surgery."

Not sure what a lesion was or what it all meant, I asked, "What kind of surgery?"

"A craniotomy."

"Craniotomy? Are you serious? Isn't there something else they can do?"

"Like what, Kathi?"

"I don't know! Something other than cutting off the top of my brother's head, Suzanne!"

Scenes from a sci-fi movie and a medical documentary flashed before my eyes, where they saw off the top of the skull and expose the entire brain. I felt a wave of nausea. My skin turned hot and flushed.

"Kathi, it's not going to be like that. They think the lesion on the side of his head is causing the seizures. They will cut a tiny area near his temple, remove the tumor, and patch him up."

"What about the lesion on the top of his head?"

Her voice sank to a whisper, "That one is inoperable."

Cold terror bludgeoned me as I sank to the floor. Carole dropped beside me.

On February 1, 1995, our mother's birthday, my brother Jeff had a craniotomy.

I don't remember how long they kept him in the hospital.

I don't remember when they told me there were more tumors in his brain.

I don't remember when they told me he had tumors in his lung.

I don't remember when they told me he had tumors in his liver.

I don't remember when they told me all the tumors were metastatic cancer.

I don't remember when they told me it was stage four malignant melanoma.

What I do remember is the suffocating agony with each new piece of information—shards ripping through my heart and my life bleeding through each gaping hole.

He didn't see it coming. We didn't see it coming. It wasn't fair. Not to him. Not to his bride. Not to his daughter. Not to any of the Morris orphans. Especially so soon after Michael's death.

Jeff, thirty-four, a newlywed with a home in escrow, was released from the hospital with a death sentence. The doctors and Suzanne were forthcoming with Jeff on the diagnosis and his six to twelve-month prognosis. But, he either consciously or subconsciously refused to hear it. When given his options, he consistently chose the most aggressive treatments of chemotherapy and radiation.

I was no more accepting of his condition than Jeff. I had no idea what stage four cancer meant. I needed information. I needed hope. I needed to know there was a cure. I needed to know someone else had the same diagnosis and won the fight. I needed somebody, anybody, to tell me everything would be okay. I was prepared to go to any length, to spend any amount of money, to travel anywhere on the planet to get him the help he needed. I couldn't take another loss. Especially not my sweet brother, Jeffrey.

I began researching the internet and found the cancer society. I dialed their number, fully believing they would tell me how to help my brother. When a woman answered the phone, I began speaking earnestly, "Hello, I'm calling because I have a brother that was diagnosed with stage four malignant melanoma. He has tumors in his brain, liver, and lung. I am hoping you can tell me where to get the best medical care."

I waited for her response, confident she would give me the information I needed to help my brother. All hope was shattered with her sincere and compassionate response of, "I am so sorry!"

Genuinely confused, I asked, "What do you mean?"

"When cancer is that far advanced, the prognosis is usually not very good. I wish there was something I could say to help you."

I hung up the phone, scared and confused. On a freefall—I was frantically searching for a safety net. A Hail Mary. Not a slap of reality. Not someone to tell me the gravity of his illness and offer no help. Still, I remained steadfast in my determination to hold on to miracles.

With nowhere else to turn, I turned to God. I never prayed so hard in my life. I said Rosaries. I spent my lunch hour at St John's Cathedral attending Mass. Every day at home, I got down on my knees, lifted my head, stretched my arms toward the sky, and screamed, "God! You said if I had the faith of a mustard seed that I could move mountains! I do have the faith of a mustard seed! Nothing is impossible with You! I know you can cure Jeffrey! You can't take him so soon after Mike! Please, God, I'm begging you to heal Jeffrey!"

Despite my devout prayers, Jeff continued to have seizures, lost his hair, and began to lose weight. Jeff, despite the aggressive treatments, tried his best to maintain a normal life. So when his longtime friend asked him to be the best man at his wedding, he readily accepted. Jeff understood the six-hour drive to Fresno in the middle of radiation treatments would be difficult, but he was up for the challenge. I eagerly offered my home for their stay.

When Jeff stepped out of the car, other than his shaved head, he didn't look much different to me. Family and friends dropped by to see him. We maintained the same upbeat atmosphere with music and shooting pool. If he was tired or hurting, he did a great job hiding it. He was the same Jeff to us—laughing and slinging his familiar one-liners and Jeffisms.

That night, I asked the family to gather in the great room. The great room, with its thirty-five-foot high rough-sawn ceiling, oak entertainment center, and slate fireplace, was our frequent dance and music hall. One by one, Suzanne and April; my sisters Linda, Carole, Theresa, and Roberta; my kids, Cherise and Ryan; my husband Larry; Jeff, and I shuffled into the room. We stood in a circle holding hands while Jeff sat on the fireplace hearth. I turned on his favorite song, "Tick Tock," and we all began to sing. For Jeff, it appeared we were singing along with the music. In reality, we were singing our devotion to Jeff through tear-filled eyes.

The wedding was the next day. While I was cleaning up food and trash from the night before, I heard a bedroom door open. Jeff, dressed in his black tux and shades, strutted across the room. When he reached the great room wall, without saying a word, he swung around and struck a Blues Brothers pose. I laughed hysterically and died a little at the same time—the thought of losing him ever-present in my mind. I held on to every word, every look, every hug, every single cell of Jeffrey.

At the wedding reception, all of us sisters sat at a round table, covered in a crisp white linen tablecloth on the green manicured lawn. When the DJ called the wedding party to the dance floor and began playing the song "Unforgettable" by Nat King Cole, we all lost it.

Carole and I created a video two years earlier for all of our siblings. We converted the eight-millimeter films that Dad recorded of our childhood and photos from our family album to VHS. We enhanced the video with voiceovers and music. We used the song "Unforgettable" for the pictures of our mother. From that day forward, every time we heard that song, we were reduced to tears. When the first four bars of the music began playing and Jeff stepped onto the dance floor, we looked around at each other, and on cue, began sobbing.

When the music ended, Jeff looked our way and saw our faces smeared with mascara and blowing our noses. Jeff, our protector, made his way through the crowd toward us. When he reached our table, he shook his head, and with his signature look, said, "You weirdos—what is your problem?" We laughed through our tears.

↤

After the wedding, Jeff returned to Las Vegas to continue treatments. In July, Suzanne asked him how he felt about vacationing at his beloved Dinkey Creek. Nothing had been more telling of his decline than when he admitted he didn't have the strength to sustain a week roughing it at his beloved Camp Fresno. He suggested we stay at Shaver Lake, thirteen miles east of Dinkey Creek. In stark contrast to our summer before, where we spread out in three cabins, twelve of us shared a two-story, five-bedroom house with all the comforts of home. It was as if we needed to huddle together to embrace each other.

Carole's family and mine waited for Jeff and his family at the cabin. I tried my best to hide my shock when Jeff stepped out of the car. Only three months had passed since I saw him at the wedding, yet he was noticeably thinner and weak.

Jeff slept most of the time in the knotty pine bedroom on the first floor. I checked on him lying on top of an Americana quilt, his arms folded across his chest, and had the disturbing thought, *that's what he's going to look like in his coffin.* I understood he was fighting for his life. What I didn't understand was how the craniotomy and treatments affected him until one day he and I were alone.

I took him for a leisurely drive around the lake while everyone else went horseback riding. Everything seemed perfect that day—the weather, the sapphire lake reflecting the rays of the noonday sun, and the sweet aromatic smell of pine trees. Overcome with deep appreciation, I said, "I'm so glad you're here, Jeff. I know how hard it must have been to make that long drive."

"Getting here wasn't that hard. Suzanne drove the entire way. I'm just bummed that I don't have any energy."

"I understand, but you seem to be yourself otherwise."

"No, I'm not the same. I can't think straight."

"It doesn't seem that way! I haven't noticed any difference."

"I can't explain it, but it's little things, like I can't remember words. Or when I'm trying to tell somebody something, I can't think of how to say it."

"We all do that, Jeff. I think you're fine."

"I don't think so. Remember when Mike said after his motor-cycle accident that he wasn't the same? He said he knew he had brain damage?"

"Yes, but he always joked about it and called it 'drain bamage.'"

"He joked about it because it bothered him. He knew it was true. I understand what he meant now."

What could I say? Jeff believed something to be true that I couldn't see or understand. At least not that day. The next day I understood. We sisters were on the outside deck sweeping brown pine needles and yellow pollen off the wooden picnic tables to prepare dinner. Carole put Jeff's beloved song "Tick Tock" into the boombox. He loved it so much that he had it as his message on his answering machine. Jeff walked outside, listened to the music for a minute, squinted, and asked, "What song is this?" We girls turned our faces away, then ran inside so he couldn't see us cry.

The last time I saw my brother was on that vacation in July 1995. Unable to work since his craniotomy, Jeff's life revolved around doctors, treatments, and resting at home. He and I stayed in touch via the phone. Suzanne called while he slept to give me updates on his condition. She assured me that she and the doctors had been explicit with his diagnosis and terminal prognosis, and she was frustrated that Jeff did not hear them. It wasn't clear to me if he could not comprehend because of his surgery and treatments or if he was in denial.

As the weeks progressed, it became agonizingly more challenging to hold onto hope. It was evident he was declining despite the aggressive treatments because his seizures continued. He lost a lot of weight and slept most of the time. In late September, when the doctors suggested hospice, we knew the end was near. I made my routine call to Jeff.

"Hi Jeff, I'm just calling to check on you. How are you doing?"

His voice sounded weak. "I'm doing the same except last night I saw Mom and Dad."

A chill ran through me. *He saw Mom and Dad? Oh my God, how close is he to dying?*

"You did? How did that make you feel?"

"I was scared." *My poor brother. He is fighting so hard.*

He continued. "And last week, when I went to the doctor, he pissed me off."

"Why?"

"Because they want hospice to come to my house. I don't know what hospice is, but I don't need anyone coming over."

"Jeff, are you sure nobody explained to you what hospice is?"

"Yes, I'm sure."

"I thought Suzanne and your doctor explained all this to you."

"No, they didn't explain anything."

A long pause followed as I grappled with what to say. It hurt me to hear how confused Jeff was. He sounded frustrated. I gripped the phone harder as I paced in the great room.

"Do you want me to tell you?"

"Yes! I do!"

I tilted my head up as if a script would miraculously appear on the ceiling, and I could read it to him. *I don't want to do this on the phone. I don't know if I should say anything.*

"Don't you remember when Grandma was sick, and they brought in people to help take care of her?"

"Yes, but she was dying."

Oh my God, he still doesn't get it. My chest heaved as I clutched the phone harder, closed my eyes, and struggled to find the right words.

"Jeff. You know I believe in miracles and the power of prayer, right?"

"Yes, I know that."

"I don't know how to tell you this. I wish I were there right now. Do you remember when you had the craniotomy?"

"Yes."

"After your operation, they only gave you six months."

I waited for his response through the deafening silence. As the seconds ticked away, my anxiety mounted, and my heart screamed regret. I desperately wanted to rewind the last minute and retract everything I said.

When he finally spoke, his two words split me open. "To...live?"

I covered the phone to muffle the whimpers escaping my lips. And when I heard him begin to cry, my heart exploded as if it been blown out with a 12 gauge, leaving nothing but a gaping hole. Consumed in guilt, choking on tears, I repeated, "I am so sorry, Jeffrey. I love you so much."

I hung up the phone hemorrhaging with remorse and regret.

Early October, Jeff was admitted to the hospital and told there was nothing more they could do. On October 9, on his death bed, Suzanne brought champagne, and they toasted to their second wedding anniversary.

I had one final call with my sweet baby brother before he slipped into a coma.

"I love you, Jeff! Forever!"

"I love you, Kathi. Forever!"

It was eight short months from Jeff's diagnosis until his death on Oct. 22, 1995. The day a bright light was extinguished from the hearts of everyone who knew him. He fought valiantly to the end, not once believing or accepting that he was dying.

"Go Rest High on That Mountain" played softly as family and friends gathered in St. Paul Newman Center for his funeral. A table placed at the front of the church, draped with Jeff's childhood blanket of violet flowers, held a picture of Jeff, perched on a rock at his holy grail, Dinkey Creek. Beside it, a wooden box, engraved with an alpine scene of majestic pine trees and mountains, contained Jeff's remains.

Our brother was thirty-five when he died.

Our mother was thirty-five when she died.

We buried him with our mother.

Jeff's headstone, Calvary Cemetery, Madera, California

Jeff, 8, Madera

Jeff's Senior Picture, Class of 1978,
Clovis High School, Clovis, California

Jeff and Suzanne's wedding, Las Vegas, Nevada, Oct. 9, 1993

Jeff and his daughter April clowning around

Jeff at his beloved Dinkey Creek the year before he died, 1994

Jeff's Blues Brothers pose while preparing for his friend's wedding, April 1, 1995

Jeff's funeral, St. Paul Newman Center, Fresno, California, Oct. 27, 1995

Feb 27, 1970

Dear Kathy

I'am okay. Thank you for all of the
things you gave to me, those things are so
cool, I wish I could have gone there to that
museum. Just seeing things from it sounds neat
This is what I got for Xmas, I got a army
hat, a pistol, a pack to carry things in, and a
gerned. I got a bran new coat It is a nice
blue. I got a pop gun, a little doll like, and
it sticks, it's tung eut, it's real cool. I got a
Hot wheel car it's orange. Some undershirts. This what
I got from grandma and grandpa and aunt mary, I got
a bank a Dollar to put in my bank, I got some
pants and a shirt from Uncle Steve, the shirt
is blue, and the paints are black. Thats what I
got. How was It at the Beach, I bet I was
fun to take all those things out of the water.
Realy got wet when you fell into the water,
I bet those little dogs are quit, I wish I had
one of them. If I had a chose I would take the
little white one. When you read my letter I don't
think you understud, We had to wear ripped close
to a Basket Ball game not to a 4-H meeting.
Guess what tomomorw at the fairgrounds theres going
to be a horse show, were going to go. Roberta stopped
because she didn't like to goto the meetings, she
got sick of them, she hates them, I think there
fun to go to. Well I can't think of any thing
to say so good-by for now

Love you a lot
Jeff you best brother

P.S. Write back fast please. GOOD-BY→

Letter from Jeff, 10, Feb. 27, 1970

Dear Roberta,   Oct. 16, 1975

Hey Dude! whats happening?
I got your letter a couple of weeks
ago. It sure made me feel good to get
a letter from you. Schools pretty good
this year. I sorta like it better this
year because I know whats going on
and we can screw around more. I'm
an old coward at it now (Get it!*)
I know, your not laughing. Sounds like
you have alot of tests. Poor kid. The
rest of this letter is confidental; don't
tell a soul about this. For the last
three weeks every Friday and saturday
night. A bunch of guys and me have
been going out drinking under this bridge
We've been having a bad old time.
The faculty doesn't know shit about it;
the dumb suckers. Another thing you
can't tell. The principal called me into
his office one night and told me the
Faculty was all pissed off about the
way I've been acting, and my attitude.
They said I mess around in class, cop
an all kinds of guys, give the teachers
a bad time in class; beat up on the
Freshmen, and come late to classes
with out a reason. They said they

took a vote in the faculty meeting
about wether kicking me out and
over half of the faculty voted yes.
But, the principal said we would give
him one more chance and he would
talk to me. The principal said If
they get one more complaint they
won't vote or talk to me or anything
they will just kick me out. I
don't care, I'm getting sick of this
school. They think I'm scared. They
can suck eggs for all I care.
I'll see when I come home for
Thanksgiving, that's in about 40
days. Well thats about it for now
Take care, Don't let those big bugs
pick up on you.

                              Love, Always
                              Jeff

P.S. Thanks for the compliment about how
sharp looking I am. You did have to
tell that anyway. Shit Man, Tell
Carolyn Hi and I love her. Tell
everybody else Hi!
xo xo XO   Roberta
                    ↑   XO
       Carolyn   not   Berta
                   really.
                   Im
                   just
                   Kidding

Letter from Jeff to our sister Roberta when he was 15 and attending
St. Anthony's Seminary, Santa Barbara, California, Oct. 1975 (2 pages)

Chapter 28

CHICAGO LITHUANIANS AND THE MOB

M<sup>y mother was a product of her Lithuanian upbringing in Chicago, Illinois. My maternal great-grandparents who immigrated from Germany had little influence on her compared to that of my great paternal grandfather, Stephen Lachawicz. Born in Lithuania in 1874, he boarded the SS Noorland to escape poverty, religious persecution, and Soviet rule and arrived in New York in 1900. He made his way to Chicago, as did thousands of other Lithuanians. Referred to as the second capital, more Lithuanians lived in Chicago than any of their homeland towns.

Their size and strength allowed Lithuanians to maintain a sense of their ethnic culture. Children were expected to attend Lithuanian Saturday school to keep the language and customs of their ancestry alive. Male domination was a given, as was the rigid set of beliefs about women's roles. Primarily Roman Catholic, they built infrastructure, including churches that glued the community together. Children's summer camps, choirs, dancing troupes, Scouts, arts, and sports were encouraged. Dating within their ethnic group was expected.

My great grandfather married another Lithuanian, Victoria Kislauskis. Together they had five children. My mother's father, my grandfather, Bolislaus, was born in 1907. His mother died in 1921 when he was fourteen.

In 1916, my great grandfather opened a funeral home on 2314 W. 23rd Place, in the lower west side of Chicago. The family lived on the second floor. The S. D. Lachawicz funeral parlor was strategically located across the street from Our Lady of Vilna Catholic Church. All Lithuanians who attended that church used his funeral home for their burial services.

The funeral home became a community center. People visited wakes of people they hardly knew to socialize and meet others in the neighborhood. Everyone had calendars from the funeral home hanging on their walls. Some had wooden folding chairs in their homes with the name "Lachawicz" stenciled on the back, acquired when the funeral home replaced their seating.

My grandfather, nine when the funeral home opened, helped with its operation. When old enough, he drove the hearse and later graduated from embalming school and became a funeral director. We were either intrigued or repulsed at the stories Grandpa shared about the funeral home. It was creepy to know he lived on the floor above dead bodies, and it was interesting to learn about the embalming process.

The most noteworthy funeral my grandfather officiated was for the Venerable Mother Maria Kaupas, attended by thousands. Born in Lithuania, she immigrated to America and founded the Sisters of Saint Casimir. The sisters staffed the parochial schools that my mother attended.

Grandpa met and married my grandmother, Violet Hoffmann, a German, in 1930. In 1932 her preterm daughter died within two days of birth. Pregnant again the following year with my mother, Grandma was filled with joy and named her angel Joyce Angela. She was a beautiful baby with blond hair, green eyes, and chubby rosy cheeks. Grandma had three more children: sons in 1934 and 1940, and her last daughter in 1951 when she was forty-four years old.

I would imagine that, based on Lithuanian culture, Grandpa marrying a German Protestant caused dissension within the family; however, Grandma quickly adapted to Lithuanian mores. She was subservient. She converted to Catholicism. Mom and her brothers attended Catholic schools. They took dance and music lessons. Grandma learned how to prepare Lithuanian dishes like kugelis (potato pudding), oxtail soup, and zilch—a gelatinous mix of pig's feet and vinegar.

Mom was a sickly child and was at death's door twice with pneumonia before her seventh birthday. Eventually her health improved, and Grandma passed her love for performing arts to my mother.

Grandma had a master's degree in music and taught piano at the E.V. Eggert School of Music. She introduced Mom to the piano as soon as she could reach the keys. At ten, Mom played "Malagueña" superbly. It's a technical piece that requires great passion and control. However, it was dance that Mom loved most. She began lessons when she was five, joined a dance troupe, and had ambitions to become a prima ballerina.

I loved looking at the professional studio photographs taken of her dance troupe in their costumes. Toy soldiers in tap shoes. Girls in ballet slippers with their faces framed in flower petals as they posed within a garden fence. But my most favorite was her toe pictures with her dance partner. One of the photos was published in the newspaper with the following caption:

> *Joanne Ambrosino (left) and Joyce Lachawicz are members of a group of dancers on the entertainment program arranged for the Welcome Home Banquet for returned servicemen to be given tonight by the Holy Name Society of All Saint's Church.*

It was the end of WWII, 1946. She was thirteen years old.

Mom, 13, on the right, publicity shot, Chicago, Illinois, 1946

Mom, 13, on the left, Chicago, Illinois, 1946

My great-grandfather opened a second funeral home on 10756 S. Michigan, Chicago, in the 1940s. My grandparents, Mom, and her two brothers lived on the top floor. The boys would hide in coffins to scare each other and their friends. To combat the overpowering odor of formaldehyde, they stopped to smell the gardenias growing outside the back door before stepping inside.

Eventually, my grandparents bought a house in Southside, Chicago. They were the stereotypical Chicagoans—loud, blunt, and assertive. They had lavish birthday parties and took family vacations in Wisconsin, Michigan, and Cedar Lake, Illinois. By all accounts, they lived a comfortable and respectable upper-middle-class life in a home filled with music.

So why then, in 1947, did my forty-year-old grandfather, married, with three children, leave a lucrative family business and move to California?

My grandmother told me Grandpa was on the verge of a nervous breakdown. The stress from his strained relationship with his father caused large patches of his hair to fall out. Even as an adult, his father would hit him on the head with his cane. Grandpa saw a doctor for his nerves, who advised him to move.

It is colorful speculation that another factor may have played a role in their decision to move. Aunt Mary, my grandparent's youngest daughter, said Grandpa bootlegged for Al Capone. I never questioned Grandpa, but there is compelling evidence it could be true.

Lithuanian men were heavy drinkers. They drank to drown the sorrows of the life they left behind and to ease the pain of hard labor in the Chicago stockyards and steel mills. However, the consumption of alcohol was pushed underground when Prohibition, the nation-wide ban on the production, transportation, and sale of alcohol, was enacted from 1920–1933.

The Chicago Outfit, led by one of the most infamous gangsters in history, Al Capone, originated in Southside Chicago and rose to power in the 1920s. The greatest source of income for the mafia was from illegal liquor. They distributed alcohol to speakeasies, restaurants, and retail outlets. What better way to transport illicit liquor than in an unsuspecting hearse during the black of night? Grandpa could have been driving the hearse as early as 1920, when he was thirteen. He indeed drove it during the last ten years of prohibition. His nicknames—Bully, Digger, and Blackie—might have been a double entendre.

The whole truth of why Grandpa left Chicago will remain family lore. It's me asking the hard questions and trying to make sense of something that doesn't make sense. Socially, culturally, and financially the move was a significant step down. They sold their home, bought a 1947 Plymouth, a thirty-three-foot house trailer, and drove for ten days to California. Their trek ended in a trailer park in Calwa—a small town on the southern outskirts of Fresno. Grandpa worked maintenance for the railroad, and Grandma found a job as a maid at Hotel California.

Anyone and everyone who knows the truth died long ago. But one thing's for sure: the mafia kept the funeral parlors in business with their bloody gang wars. Capone was widely assumed to have ordered the 1929 St. Valentine's Day Massacre that left seven gang members dead. I would imagine anyone who crossed Capone or knew something incriminating would be fearful … or stressed.

Chapter 29

JOYCE ANGELA

My grandparents made many sacrifices when they moved to California in 1947, including trading their spacious home for a trailer with two hundred forty square feet of living space; however, they were not willing to compromise their children's education. When they moved to Calwa, they enrolled my fourteen-year-old mother in San Joaquin Memorial Catholic High School (SJM) in Fresno. Too far to commute, she lived in the boarding house on the grounds of SJM. The same boarding house I lived in twenty years later.

In 1949, my grandparents sold their trailer and bought a house. It was then that my sixteen-year-old mother moved home with her family. They might have regretted that decision.

Mom and her fifteen-year-old brother decided to throw a party while my grandparents were out for the evening. They naively believed that hanging signs all over Fresno advertising the date, start, and end time would operate like birthday invitations and attract a manageable group of teenagers. They soon discovered a mob does not adhere to the rules.

Nobody knows how many hundreds of people converged on their home and surrounding streets that night. People were shoulder to shoulder, and cars were parked so tight that walking on top of them became the only exit. My grandparents returned home to trash, liquor bottles, and revelers roaming the street.

I can only guess how angry my grandparents were. I'm sure punishment came fast and furious. I am just as confident the drunken euphoria of young love eclipsed its sting. For it was on that fortuitous night, a James Dean lookalike with a ducktail haircut and black leather jacket stole Mom's heart. Lovestruck, she succumbed to his charming wiles. It was a story reminiscent of the movie *Dirty Dancing*—the educated and cultured young girl smitten by the bad boy from across the tracks.

Mom and Dad continued to date, but when my mother said she wanted to move away to attend an out-of-town college, my father tried to discourage her. The decisive moment arrived in the form of motherhood.

Mom was seventeen and pregnant with me when she graduated from high school in 1950. When my grandparents found out, they wasted no time whisking my parents to Reno for a shotgun wedding.

My mother spent the rest of her life having babies. She had a girl every year for the first five years: Me, Judy, Linda, Carole, and Theresa. She skipped a year and had twins, Robert and Roberta. Dad was elated—after six daughters, he finally had a son. Mike was born the following year; Jeff, two years later; and Eddie five years after that. There are fourteen years between my youngest brother and me.

Our large family was a curious sight to most people, and they had no qualms asking Mom questions such as, "Are all those kids yours? How many are there? How old are you?" The drill became as routine and predictable as her having a baby every year.

I enjoyed her playful side when she jumped rope or played hopscotch with us. I was nine years old when Mom shocked me by doing a perfect three-point handstand. That agile feat of strength peeled back my view of her as a baby factory. Producing children was her claim to fame—like a gold medal she wore with pride but was never allowed to remove.

Mom was 5'2". Short, but not petite. Big-boned and big-busted. Hazel eyes behind thick-lensed glasses to correct her severe nearsightedness. She had coarse, thick, sandy blond hair that she wore in a French roll or bouffant styled. Her voice and boisterous laugh were instantly identifiable. She was a beautiful woman despite her facial pock scars, which were remnants of the terrible acne cysts she suffered as a teenager. She said the cysts would burst in the freezing Chicago winters, much to her pain and embarrassment. Mom modeled for Kinney Shoes once, and the picture was featured in the local newspaper.

Mom was confident, independent, and resourceful. In 1958, she applied as a contestant on *Queen for a Day* and won. She was twenty-five, pregnant, and had seven kids. The television game show, hosted by Jack Bailey, had big prize giveaways. Four women competed by sharing their financial or emotional hardships to a live audience. They voiced what they needed most and why they wanted to win. The studio audience chose the winner with an applause meter. Who wouldn't clap for a pregnant, twenty-five-year-old struggling to maintain a household for nine people? I was too young to remember exactly what she won, but I remember the living room floor covered with many boxes possibly containing pots and pans and small appliances.

We were raised with morals, manners, and modesty. Mom disciplined us with proverbs, such as "people who live in glass houses shouldn't throw stones"; "children are to be seen and not heard"; "early to bed and early to rise, makes a man healthy, wealthy, and wise." A lot of them didn't make sense to me at the time—like who lives in a glass house?

We sat together at the dining room table for every meal, said grace, ate with our mouths closed, and did not speak while eating. I'm not sure if we weren't allowed to speak, or we didn't talk because we were too busy inhaling our food. With not much to go around, a second serving required finishing before everyone else.

Mom's aspiration to become a dietician helped with stretching a dollar and serving balanced meals. She was also a genius with leftovers. Spaghetti with margarine the first night. Spaghetti fried with scrambled eggs the next. When money was scarce, sometimes lettuce was the only thing we had for dinner. She sliced the head into quarters or eighths and smeared mayonnaise on it. Who knew it would be a chic dish today?

We didn't have expensive cuts of meat, like steak or pork chops. In the 1960s, ground beef was four pounds for a dollar. We ate it in every form imaginable—meatloaf, hamburgers, tacos, and everything in between.

Mom loved music and made sure we owned a piano. On occasion, she played her beloved "Malagueña" or invited us to sit beside her and play chopsticks. Stacks of records lined the living room, from artists such as Johnny Mathis, Frank Sinatra, and Doris Day. She loved to sing, especially while working around the house. Songs like "How Much is that Doggie in the Window?" and "We're Off to See the Wizard." Mom had a wistful look and grace about her as she sang her favorite song, "Que Sera Sera."

The album *Sing Along with Mitch* was a family favorite. We kids knew every song by heart and sang them loud and proud: "By the Light of the Silvery Moon" and "Down by the Old Mill Stream." Some of our favorite moments were dancing to the records. We would blast the music and pair up—a big kid with a little kid, or two big kids. We screamed with laughter and stepped on each other's toes as we circled the living room doing the polka.

Our mother did not drink, smoke, or do drugs. Her only vice was Pepsi. I don't know if I would call it an addiction, but close to it. The bottles containing the sweet, fizzy dark soda were always around. She bought several six-packs at a time and drank at least six bottles a day. Our job was to return the empty bottles to the grocery store to retrieve the deposit and buy more Pepsi. It was a challenging and formidable balancing act requiring two kids. We piled a mountain of bottles in our red radio flyer wagon and pulled it for blocks on uneven side-walks. One pulled, the other lifted the back end of the wagon when we reached a curb. God forbid we drop a bottle coming or going.

Mom had an irrational fear of frogs. If she saw one on television, she bolted from the living room, screaming. You can imagine how trau-matized she was for the six months we lived in a Los Angeles home we aptly named "the frog house." Every night giant, green, croaking frogs blanketed the front lawn. Mom stood paralyzed at the front door or sat in the car until we cleared a path for her to run. I'm not sure if we moved after six months because Kinney Shoes transferred our father again, or because my mother put her foot down.

Mom had a great sense of humor. Unfortunately, I was the butt of one of her shenanigans in 1965. She took Aunt Mary and me to Ratcliffe Stadium in Fresno to see a Rolling Stones concert. We were fourteen, self-conscious, and boy crazy. Hundreds of teenagers lined the chain-link fence where Mom dropped us off. Aunt Mary and I stepped out of the car styling in our red and blue madras shirts. As soon as I got out, my nose began to run. Pounding on the car window, I yelled, "Mom! Stop the car!"

"What do you want?" she yelled back.

"Open the window! I need a Kleenex. Do you have any?"

"No, but this should work!" As she pulled away, she threw a Kotex out the window. It landed on the ground in full view of everyone standing in line. She sped off, cackling while I died of embarrassment.

My mother was a blend of Grace Kelly and Lucille Ball. Gracious, sophisticated, and refined countered with a down-to-earth brassiness and sometimes sauciness. When I recoiled after she explained how to have sex, her coy response was, "Don't knock it till you try it!"

She had that unique ability to connect and converse with anyone regardless of their position or status. She met Nancy Reagan at a political fundraiser when Ronald Reagan ran for the presidential nomination in 1968. Somehow she managed to have a one-on-one conversation with her. I was impressed she had the wherewithal to talk to Nancy Reagan. I was also taken aback by her animated enthusiasm when sharing their discussion. In place of my mother, I saw an intellect that shed the oppressive cloak of domestic drudgery.

⌣

As a child, I didn't give our expanding family much thought or question my mother's judgment when she said she wanted an even dozen.

A houseful of kids was all I ever knew. When I became a teenager and examined the size of our family through a more mature lens, I asked her, "Mom! Why did you have so many kids?"

Busy pressing Dad's white dress shirt, with a can of starch in one hand and an iron in the other, she responded, "Because I love babies."

"Yeah, well, babies grow up!"

"I know. That's the problem!" She further explained that as a Catholic, the only acceptable birth control was abstinence or the rhythm method. Laughing, she continued, "Obviously, neither method is working for us."

I was thirteen when Mom invited me to go to the grocery store with her. I found it odd that she asked me to join her, but, always happy to get out of the house, I agreed.

We were strolling through the aisle of canned goods when she suddenly announced, "Don't tell your father, but I am going to have another baby!"

"Really? I am so excited! I can't wait!" I shrieked while jumping up and down.

"You are?" She was genuinely surprised by my reaction.

"Yeah, it's been a long time since we had a baby in the house!" Jeff, the youngest, was four years old. The longest stretch we ever had between babies was two years.

"I don't think your father will be as enthusiastic, so don't you tell anyone!"

In 1965, Mom gave birth to her tenth and last child. During that pregnancy, she was diagnosed with diabetes and closely monitored because of the baby's size. My youngest brother was delivered by cesarean in the eighth month and weighed over eleven pounds. Mom named him Edward Vincent after her heartthrob—the actor Vincent

Edwards. She also conceded to a hysterectomy as advised by her doctor. Mom was heartbroken. She really did want a dozen children.

Mom probably had diabetes for years. One of the symptoms is excessively heavy newborns. The twins weighed over eight pounds each. Mom's belly was so big, she used it as a table to balance her dinner plate. She did not drive because she couldn't fit behind the wheel. Mike and Jeff, both born after the twins, weighed over nine and ten pounds each.

Her baby manufacturing days behind her, raising teenagers was next on the list.

First up, her firstborn.

Me.

Chapter 30

DANCING
WITH ANGELS

I t's been over fifty years since my mother died. I want to honor her but still tell my truth. The truth is, she and I did not have the best relationship. At the time of her death, I was seventeen and becoming rebellious. However, as an adult looking back, I still feel she had me at an arm's length. I did not feel loved. Our goodnight kisses stopped when I became a teenager. I don't recall her hugging me—ever. My earliest memory is her chasing me around the house to hit me.

Mom saddled me with adult responsibilities from an early age. I was seven years old the first time she left me alone to babysit my six siblings, including one-year-old twins. The hour felt like an eternity and left me traumatized. I heard sounds outside, and in my little-girl mind, they came from a burglar walking on the roof. I was sobbing when Mom returned, and when I told her a robber was trying to break in, she laughed.

As I grew older, my responsibilities grew. My position description as the oldest child included setting the example for my siblings. I was expected to earn straight As, cook, clean, and do the laundry. I morphed into a surrogate mother in every sense of the word.

Mom was spread too thin to attach to us as individuals, at least not to me. I didn't believe she had feelings until I turned nine. One day as I was washing dishes, the garage door flung open, and Mom bolted into the house crying hysterically. She accidentally ran over our puppy and killed it. I was genuinely shocked that it affected her.

My mother could be polite and proper one day, holding manners in her hand like a second skin. The next day she was cursing like a sailor. "Kathi, Judy, Linda, Carole, Theresa, Roberta, Robert, Michael, Jeff, and Ed! Get your asses in the house before I beat the shit out of you!" It was a cattle call I grew up listening to my entire life.

Her constant yelling was abrasive and tiring. I would escape to my bedroom, cover my ears, and silently beg, *would you please shut up?* As with most mothers, two sides fight for a purpose: the fierce lioness protecting her cubs and the fire-storm making order out of chaos.

Mom ruled our routine and regimented lives with an iron fist. We followed the rules out of fear of the consequences. To talk back, lie, or disobey insured a quick backhanded slap or whipping with a belt.

For most years, our mother was a stay-at-home mom, which I preferred. I hated when she worked because I would return home from school to notes taped to the kitchen cabinet with a list of chores. The last line, in bold capital letters, read "Clean till it shines!" And she meant it! At least I thought she did, and I did not want to risk the consequences of noncompliance. The only upshot to cleaning was that there were so many of us. I assigned two kids to each room, gave them their marching orders, and inspected their work to verify it met Mom's standards. In an hour, the entire house shined.

In junior high school, my resentment at being burdened with the house and kids began to manifest itself. Driven to earn high marks because it was the only time I received praise, I was horrified when I opened my report card in seventh grade and saw mostly Cs. I braced myself for Mom's wrath as she read my report card. No amount of corporal punishment would have dealt the same blow as when she said, "I was starting to feel sorry for you, for leaving you home with all the kids...but not now."

She had feelings for me? Hearing those words, my spirit leaped for joy. Hope springs eternal, especially when the unrequited love involves your mother. When she followed her statement with, "But not now," despair, my constant companion, replaced my moment of happiness.

My punishment, a visit to the school counselor, crippled me with embarrassment because I was painfully shy. In school, I did everything in my power to avoid bringing attention to myself. After the counseling session, my grades improved while my self-esteem continued to suffer.

Later that year, in 1964, Mom gathered the nine of us siblings for an annihilating blow. She told us to choose who we wanted to live with because she was leaving our father. She didn't explain why. I presumed she suspected infidelity because it had happened nine years earlier.

⌐

In 1955, when Mom was pregnant and had four toddlers under age five, Dad was seeing another woman. I was four years old and too young to understand what was going on. He took me to her house once and sat me on a barstool. I remember thinking, *I don't know who she is, but she's pretty, and she sure smiles a lot.*

Dad moved out, and Grandma Lachawicz moved in. Grandma and Mom didn't know the woman's identity, but every night Mom lit candles, and we prayed the Rosary for his return. As luck or divine intervention would have it, when Grandma stopped at the neighborhood dry cleaners, the woman behind the counter initiated a conversation. She said her daughter had met a handsome and charming man who had a little girl. She also mentioned that he laid carpet for a living.

"Really? So does my son-in-law!" Grandma exclaimed.

"Which company does he work for?" the woman asked.

"Shepherd Rug Company," Grandma replied.

"Why, that's the same company Bob works for!"

"Her boyfriend's name is Bob? What's his last name?" Grandma asked.

"Morris. His name is Bob Morris."

"Oh, my God! That's my son-in-law! He is married to my pregnant daughter! And he has four daughters, not one!"

For the rest of his life, Dad told everyone, "If you need a miracle, just have my wife and mother-in-law pray for you."

Dad returned home, Grandma moved out, and we went on with our lives.

⌣

Nine years later, with nine kids in tow, our mother intended to leave our father.

"All of you get in the living room. I need to talk to you," Mom said one afternoon.

When we had gathered around her, she declared, "I am going to leave your father. Who do you want to live with? Him or me?"

The nine of us began wailing in unison. She looked at me and asked, "Why are you crying?"

I was thirteen, confused and devastated. *I have to choose between my mother or my father? Am I supposed to live with one of them and not the other?* Although I was a daddy's girl, the thought of not having my mother was too much to accept. "No! I am not going to choose! I don't want you to leave Dad!"

Her puzzled expression lingered long after the nine of us stopped crying. I don't know if my father knew how she crushed us that afternoon, leaving me anxious and scared. Interestingly, she became pregnant with my youngest brother, her tenth child, soon after that day.

In 1966, I was fifteen when Mom had emergency surgery for a kidney stone. Bedridden for four days with a temperature of 105 and writhing in pain, her friend Jane came over and knew something was seriously wrong. Jane called our father to tell him she was taking Mom to the hospital.

On her way to the car, Mom spewed obscenities at me. Nothing she said made sense. I learned later that Mom was delirious because of the fever, but her attack hurt me deeply. In a house full of people, she directed her vitriol toward me only. I refused to visit her for the week that she was hospitalized. She asked Dad why, and when he explained what she had done, she still refused to apologize.

When I was sixteen, our struggle came to a head. On a frigid night in January, Mom said, "Put on your coat, Kathi. We are going for a ride."

"Where are we going?" I asked.

"To Fresno," she responded.

"Why?"

"Just put on your coat and get in the car."

Her sharp tone left no doubt I was in trouble. My parents and I rode in icy silence for the half-hour drive. When my dad pulled into the driveway of my grandparents' house, I was more confused than ever.

Aunt Mary still lived with Grandma and Grandpa. She and I were the same age and hung around together. When we entered the house, Mom instructed Aunt Mary and me to sit on the white sofa in the living room while the adults talked in the kitchen.

"What's going on?" Aunt Mary asked when they were out of earshot.

"I have no idea. But I think we're in trouble for something." I motioned for her to lower her voice.

"Then you better let me do all the talking," Aunt Mary suggested.

She had a Ph.D. in quick thinking and lying, so I agreed.

My parents and grandparents stepped out of the kitchen and made their way into the living room. They stood glaring at us with their hands on their hips. My mother began firing questions while Aunt Mary responded.

"So what did you girls do at the concert the other night?" Mom asked with narrowed eyes.

"Danced and talked to our friends," Aunt Mary responded calmly.

"Anything else we should know about?"

The four adults began to fidget, crossed their arms, and adjusted their weight from one foot to another.

"Umm, not really," Aunt Mary said and looked over at me. I still had no clue, so I did not react.

"Did you see Rod?" Rod was Aunt Mary's boyfriend.

"Yes." My aunt responded while straightening her posture.

"Did he give you something?" Mom's face was turning red.

"Something like what?" Aunt Mary asked.

"Something like marijuana, Mary." She enunciated the name Mary as if to add an exclamation point. I knew with that last remark my mother had read my diary.

During the 1960s, many teenagers were experimenting with drugs. My initiation into the big league happened three days earlier at a concert at the Rainbow Ballroom in downtown Fresno. That night Rod gave Aunt Mary a joint. He'd already smoked half of it, so he gave her a roach clip too. It was all curious to me because I'd never been around drugs. I was surprised to learn she had smoked pot before.

I followed Aunt Mary into a bathroom stall, where she explained what to do—inhale and hold in the smoke. She lit up, took a drag, held her breath, and handed it to me. I followed suit, inhaled, tried to hold it in, but coughed it all out. Although I had been smoking cigarettes, to inhale and hold in the smoke was a different animal. After two hits, ash hung from the clip, and it was clear that the joint was too small to have any effect on us. The only ones who knew about that night were Aunt Mary, Rod, and my diary.

The ride home was unbearably silent, interrupted only by the slap of the tires hitting the pavement. I knew I would be grounded for the rest of my life. Had I gotten stoned, the punishment might have fit the crime. As far as I was concerned, I did nothing wrong, so my nervousness teetered with the indignation of my mother invading my personal space.

I had been at odds with my sister Judy, a year younger than me, for most of my high school years. I believed she was Mom's favorite and that they most likely read my diary together. She and I shared a bedroom along with two other sisters. As soon as we arrived home, I marched to our bedroom, called Judy names, and told her how much I hated her. It erupted into a screaming match that brought my parents running.

Dad tried to mediate while I yanked open the top drawer of my heavy white wooden dresser and feverishly dug through my clothes. Tucked in the back was my small blue treasured book, MY DIARY etched in gold across the top. A sacred birthday gift from a fifth-grade friend, where I recorded my heart's desires, delights, and dreams for seven years.

My hand gripped the binding as I stomped into the living room to the fireplace and sat down on the hardwood floor in front of the roaring fire. I began tearing out every page, one by one. As I pitched the papers into the flames, my mind churned. *How could she? What else did she read? Has she read it before? I am so pissed off at her. This is my diary!*

Dad lowered himself beside me, "Kathi, please stop. I know how much your diary means to you."

"No! I will not give her the chance to do it again! I hate her! And Judy!" My mother could hear me, but I didn't care.

"Kathi, it was wrong, but you don't mean that!"

"Yes, I do. She hates me! She always has."

"Please!" Dad pled. "Go talk to your mother and apologize."

I had no intention of apologizing. I was the one wronged. I was the one who deserved an apology! After a few minutes of his pleading, I reluctantly agreed, but not before one final act of defiance. With a flick of my wrist, I tossed the remainder of my childhood confidences into the inferno and stood up.

Placing one foot in front of the other, I crossed through the darkened living room lit only by the growling fire. When I reached the arched doorway to the kitchen, my mother, in a green robe, leaned against the kitchen sink, glaring out the window. She did not attempt to look at me. Her arms hung at her sides, like a cold statue in heavy armor. I told myself, *just three more steps. You need to do this for Dad.*

I made my way across the kitchen and nervously wrapped my arms around her waist. My chest heaved as I murmured, "I'm sorry."

She didn't budge or make any attempt to reciprocate my hug. She said nothing as if her tongue was paralyzed. Impaled, I dropped my arms and stepped back as my heart bled out and my self-worth pooled on the thin linoleum floor.

Her lack of responsiveness validated everything I'd always believed. She hated me. For sixteen years, our relationship had been a constant tug of war, with me on the losing end. My craving for her love and affection drained dry; I went to bed defeated.

The next day, generated by a sense of nothing to lose, I declared, "I think I will call you Joyce from now on."

"Go ahead." Her response was cold and biting.

"You don't care?" I expected some form of rebuttal or reprisal.

"Nope!"

I called her Joyce from that day forward and began counting down the days to high school graduation when I could break free from the chains that bound me.

༆

My parents made it clear that going to college was mandatory. In June 1968, after I completed my junior year in high school, I began summer classes at Fresno City College. I wanted to get an early start on my degree by completing the required courses.

I enrolled in Sociology and Psychology and was instantly fascinated with the science of mind and behavior. I returned home from class, excited to tell my mother that I had decided on my career path—I wanted to become a psychiatrist. She responded with, "No, you're not. I don't need you analyzing me."

Three weeks later, she was dead.

Ironically, over fifty years later, I am analyzing my mother... and myself.

Perhaps our similarities created our separation. After Mom died, her best friend Jane said she had to watch herself when talking to me. My voice and mannerisms were so similar to my mother's that she thought she was talking to her.

Perhaps Mom harbored resentment because getting pregnant with me destroyed her dream to become a prima ballerina or graduate from college as a dietician.

Perhaps the demands of a husband, ten children, and running a household left little time for nurturing any of us.

Maybe I have it all wrong because I was a sensitive, emotional, and needy child.

It took spiritual growth for me to forgive my mom. It took maturity to appreciate her qualities and sacrifices. My pain is that I am an orphan. I had a mother for a mere seventeen years because a sixty-one-year-old man decided to get drunk, pop pills, and hit the highway. He robbed me of the chance to mature with my mother and possibly mend wounds and misunderstandings.

I will never know the warmth of a mother's hug or how it feels to receive a mother's kiss. I will never hear the sweet sound of a mother saying, "I love you." I will forever have an aching hole and feel I am not good enough.

My saving grace is the wisdom and insight I've gained over the years. My mother sacrificed herself for her legacy—her ten children. Did she get it all right? No, but she did the best she could with what she knew, and she did it with dignity and grace. She met the challenge and rose to the occasion every step of the way. It takes an extraordinary woman of any age to tackle the demands of raising ten children. It takes an exceptional woman to raise ten obedient and respectful children. Everything I am, I owe to my mother.

It's been over thirty years since I dreamt about my mom. In that dream, I was at a house party. While I mingled with friends, a dazzling glow from the adjoining room grabbed my attention. Captivated by the radiance and the image of something hovering in the air, I made my way through the crowd. Suspended in the center of the room, a few feet off the ground, was a woman in a long blue dress. The skirt billowed as if caught in a breeze, and a brilliant halo floated over her head. Her presence saturated the room with an indescribable calm. I moved closer, and when she lowered her ethereal face and piercing aquamarine eyes to smile at me, I realized it was my mother.

"Mom! It's you! You look so beautiful!"

She didn't speak, and she didn't look at me as much as she looked through me—infusing my soul with the serenity and knowledge that she had indeed reached her place with God.

My mother, Joyce Angela, died with the love of her life.

She died loving her babies.

She died loving me.

I love you, Mom.

Mom, 1, Chicago, Illinois, 1934

Mom in high school, San Joaquin Memorial, Class of 1950, Fresno, California

PAGE 24—Vallejo Times-Herald, Sunday, March 25, 1962

SPRING SHOE FASHIONS from Kinney's Shoes are admired by Mrs. Joyce Morris, wife of manager Bob. She has a handbag to match her new spring shoes and is looking at black patent pump which she has decided will be just the right match for her black patent handbag as accessories for the Easter parade. Handbags as well as shoes may be found among the many new Spring styles at Kinney's.

Mom, 29, Modeling for Kinney Shoes, Vallejo, California, 1962

Mom's letter to her mother, Grandma Lachawicz, three months
before she was killed, March 19, 1968 (2 pages)

My sister Judy had an entirely different relationship with our mother than I did. She and Mom were best friends. Judy allowed me to include some of her pages from a family book we composed years ago. Her pages follow....

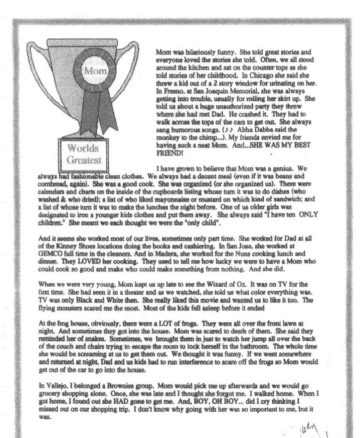

Mom was hilariously funny. She told great stories and everyone loved the stories she told. Often, we all stood around the kitchen and sat on the counter tops as she told stories of her childhood. In Chicago she said she threw a kid out of a 2 story window for urinating on her. In Fresno, at San Joaquin Memorial, she was always getting into trouble, usually for rolling her skirt up. She told us about a huge unauthorized party they threw where she had met Dad. He crashed it. They had to walk across the tops of the cars to get out. She always sang humorous songs. (♪♪ Abba Dabba said the monkey to the chimp...). My friends envied me for having such a neat Mom. And...SHE WAS MY BEST FRIEND!

I have grown to believe that Mom was a genius. We always had fashionable clean clothes. We always had a decent meal (even if it was beans and cornbread, again). She was a good cook. She was organized (or she organized us). There were calendars and charts on the inside of the cupboards listing whose turn it was to do dishes (who washed & who dried); a list of who liked mayonnaise or mustard on which kind of sandwich; and a list of whose turn it was to make the lunches the night before. One of us older girls was designated to iron a younger kids clothes and put them away. She always said "I have ten ONLY children." She meant we each thought we were the "only child".

And it seems she worked most of our lives, sometimes only part time. She worked for Dad at all of the Kinney Shoes locations doing the books and cashiering. In San Jose, she worked at GEMCO full time in the cleaners. And in Madera, she worked for the Nuns cooking lunch and dinner. They LOVED her cooking. They used to tell me how lucky we were to have a Mom who could cook so good and make who could make something from nothing. And she did.

When we were very young, Mom kept us up late to see the Wizard of Oz. It was on TV for the first time. She had seen it in a theater and as we watched, she told us what color everything was. TV was only Black and White then. She really liked this movie and wanted us to like it too. The flying monsters scared me the most. Most of the kids fell asleep before it ended

At the frog house, obviously, there were a LOT of frogs. They were all over the front lawn at night. And sometimes they got into the house. Mom was scared to death of them. She said they reminded her of snakes. Sometimes, we brought them in just to watch her jump all over the back of the couch and chairs trying to escape the room to lock herself in the bathroom. The whole time she would be screaming at us to get them out. We thought it was funny. If we went somewhere and returned at night, Dad and us kids had to run interference to scare off the frogs so Mom would get out of the car to go into the house.

In Vallejo, I belonged a Brownies group. Mom would pick me up afterwards and we would go grocery shopping alone. Once, she was late and I thought she forgot me. I walked home. When I got home, I found out she HAD gone to get me. And, BOY, OH BOY... did I cry thinking I missed out on our shopping trip. I don't know why going with her was so important to me, but it was.

Judy

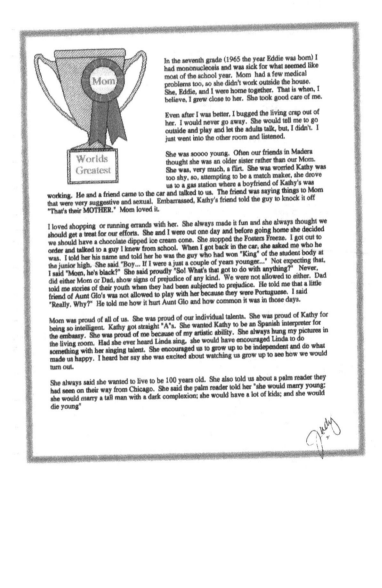

In the seventh grade (1965 the year Eddie was born) I had mononucleosis and was sick for what seemed like most of the school year. Mom had a few medical problems too, so she didn't work outside the house. She, Eddie, and I were home together. That is when, I believe, I grew close to her. She took good care of me.

Even after I was better, I bugged the living crap out of her. I would never go away. She would tell me to go outside and play and let the adults talk, but, I didn't. I just went into the other room and listened.

She was soooo young. Often our friends in Madera thought she was an older sister rather than our Mom. She was, very much, a flirt. She was worried Kathy was too shy, so, attempting to be a match maker, she drove us to a gas station where a boyfriend of Kathy's was working. He and a friend came to the car and talked to us. The friend was saying things to Mom that were very suggestive and sexual. Embarrassed, Kathy's friend told the guy to knock it off "That's their MOTHER." Mom loved it.

I loved shopping or running errands with her. She always made it fun and she always thought we should get a treat for our efforts. She and I were out one day and before going home we decided we should have a chocolate dipped ice cream cone. She stopped the Fosters Freeze. I got out to order and talked to a guy I knew from school. When I got back in the car, she asked me who he was. I told her his name and told her he was the guy who had won "King" of the student body at the junior high. She said "Boy... If I were a just a couple of years younger..." Not expecting that, I said "Mom, he's black?" She said proudly "So! What's that got to do with anything?" Never, did either Mom or Dad, show signs of prejudice of any kind. We were not allowed to either. Dad told me stories of their youth when they had been subjected to prejudice. He told me that a little friend of Aunt Glo's was not allowed to play with her because they were Portuguese. I said "Really, Why?" He told me how it hurt Aunt Glo and how common it was in those days.

Mom was proud of all of us. She was proud of our individual talents. She was proud of Kathy for being so intelligent. Kathy got straight "A"s. She wanted Kathy to be an Spanish interpreter for the embassy. She was proud of me because of my artistic ability. She always hung my pictures in the living room. Had she ever heard Linda sing, she would have encouraged Linda to do something with her singing talent. She encouraged us to grow up to be independent and do what made us happy. I heard her say she was excited about watching us grow up to see how we would turn out.

She always said she wanted to live to be 100 years old. She also told us about a palm reader they had seen on their way from Chicago. She said the palm reader told her "she would marry young; she would marry a tall man with a dark complexion; she would have a lot of kids; and she would die young"

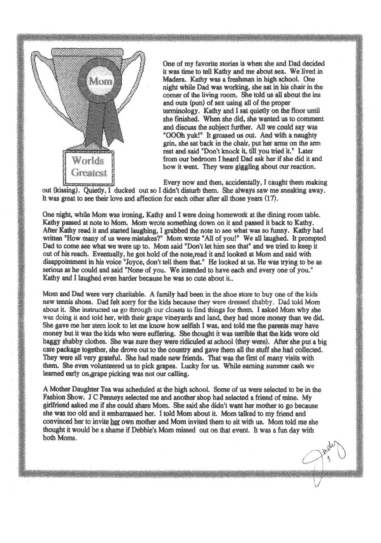

One of my favorite stories is when she and Dad decided it was time to tell Kathy and me about sex. We lived in Madera. Kathy was a freshman in high school. One night while Dad was working, she sat in his chair in the corner of the living room. She told us all about the ins and outs (pun) of sex using all of the proper terminology. Kathy and I sat quietly on the floor until she finished. When she did, she wanted us to comment and discuss the subject further. All we could say was "OOOh yuk!" It grossed us out. And with a naughty grin, she sat back in the chair, put her arms on the arm rest and said "Don't knock it, till you tried it." Later from our bedroom I heard Dad ask her if she did it and how it went. They were giggling about our reaction.

Every now and then, accidentally, I caught them making out (kissing). Quietly, I ducked out so I didn't disturb them. She always saw me sneaking away. It was great to see their love and affection for each other after all those years (17).

One night, while Mom was ironing, Kathy and I were doing homework at the dining room table. Kathy passed a note to Mom. Mom wrote something down on it and passed it back to Kathy. After Kathy read it and started laughing, I grabbed the note to see what was so funny. Kathy had written "How many of us were mistakes?" Mom wrote "All of you!" We all laughed. It prompted Dad to come see what we were up to. Mom said "Don't let him see that" and we tried to keep it out of his reach. Eventually, he got hold of the note, read it and looked at Mom and said with disappointment in his voice "Joyce, don't tell them that." He looked at us. He was trying to be as serious as he could and said "None of you. We intended to have each and every one of you." Kathy and I laughed even harder because he was so cute about it..

Mom and Dad were very charitable. A family had been in the shoe store to buy one of the kids new tennis shoes. Dad felt sorry for the kids because they were dressed shabby. Dad told Mom about it. She instructed us go through our closets to find things for them. I asked Mom why she was doing it and told her, with their grape vineyards and land, they had more money than we did. She gave me her stern look to let me know how selfish I was, and told me the parents may have money but it was the kids who were suffering. She thought it was terrible that the kids wore old baggy shabby clothes. She was sure they were ridiculed at school (they were). After she put a big care package together, she drove out to the country and gave them all the stuff she had collected. They were all very grateful. She had made new friends. That was the first of many visits with them. She even volunteered us to pick grapes. Lucky for us. While earning summer cash we learned early on, grape picking was not our calling.

A Mother Daughter Tea was scheduled at the high school. Some of us were selected to be in the Fashion Show. J C Penneys selected me and another shop had selected a friend of mine. My girlfriend asked me if she could share Mom. She said she didn't want her mother to go because she was too old and it embarrassed her. I told Mom about it. Mom talked to my friend and convinced her to invite her own mother and Mom invited them to sit with us. Mom told me she thought it would be a shame if Debbie's Mom missed out on that event. It was a fun day with both Moms.

Judy

A group of us kids had gone to a high school dance. The one guy with a car drove each of us home. My boyfriend got dropped off before I did and I was left in the car with one guy. Unexpectedly, he leaned over and kissed me. When I got home, I found Mom putting clean sheets on her bed. I grabbed one end and helped her. That had upset me and I needed to talk. I told her the whole story. I was concerned about my own boyfriend and asked her what to do. She said "Don't tell him." I told her I thought I had to. She told me "What they don't know... don't hurt 'em."

While at Madera high, I always went home for lunch. One day when I walked in the door, Mom had just gotten off of the telephone. She was very angry. I asked her what was wrong. She said "I am going to divorce your Dad! Who are you going to live with? Me or him?" Naturally, I asked her why she was so mad at him. She said "That Damn Gum! You know he doesn't have any back teeth, so, he always chews it with his front teeth and you can't understand a damn thing he says. Why doesn't he just take it out of his mouth when he knows he's going to be on the phone, anyway? He called me!" Well, I let her carry on like that for a while. And she asked me, again, to choose who I was going to live with. Then as calmly and cheerfully as I could, said "Mom... (biggg hesitation) you are going to divorce Dad for chewing gum? That's kind of funny don't you think?" I started to laugh and sensing a *hint* of a smile, continued with "My fights with my boyfriends aren't that dumb." Then, THANK GOD, she started laughing too. It wasn't often you could get away with telling Mom she was acting dumb. She was nice and calm and back to her old self before I went back to school.

When there was a Formal dance at school, she helped us shop for a dress. She made an appointment at the beauty parlor and got us there. Beforehand, we went through a ton of magazines looking for the perfect hairdo. She picked out shoes for Dad to dye the exact color of our dress. She made sure we ordered the boutonniere. She made sure the boy knew what color our dress was so the corsage matched. The day of the dance was action packed and she helped us get dressed and ready. And, she made sure we had film in the camera. She made every possible effort to make our evening special.

As we got older, she and Dad had discussions about taking us out to restaurants once in a while so they could teach us proper etiquette and social skills. They knew it was time we were going to be out in public. And they didn't want us to be embarrassed about knowing what to do with salad forks, soup spoons, sorbet and so on.... They truly cared about all aspects of our growing lives.

Judy

My sister Judy's pages about Mom taken from a family
book we compiled years ago (4 pages)

Chapter 31

ROBERT GENE

"Rise and shine, girls!" My father's voice startled me from a deep slumber.

"I'm so tired, Daddy. Can't I sleep just a little longer?" I groaned.

Giddy excitement kept me awake most of the night. Waking up at four-thirty in the morning, wrapped in darkness, felt foreign and unnatural—like crawling through a dark cave to reach sunlight.

"Not if you want to go fishing with me! Better get up and get dressed, or you're gonna get left behind!" Dad released his grip from my toes and moved to my sisters, all dead to the world. He continued shaking their toes while chanting the same reveille. We had two sets of pine bunk beds in our bedroom. The coveted top bunks were mine and Judy's while Linda and Carole slept on the bottom.

Judy, seven, the conservative, pretty sister, was not as adventurous as the rest of us. I was surprised she wanted to tag along. Linda, six, the grumpy freckle-faced sister, was best friends with five-year-old

Carole. Carole was the cheerful tomboy. They, like me, were always eager to explore. We got dressed and went looking for our father.

We found him in the kitchen where the sweet aroma of hot cocoa permeated the air. Dad twisted the lid on his stainless-steel thermos filled with instant Yuban coffee and half and half. Then he filled our thermoses with hot chocolate and handed them to us to put in our plaid red and black metal lunch boxes. "You girls grab your pillows, then get in the car. It's time to head out before the fish stop jumping!"

We giggled with excitement as we rushed to the car for our first fishing trip. Just us four girls and Dad! We piled onto the backseat and floorboard, stuffed our pillows under our heads, and tried to catch a few more winks. The road seemed endless and spooky, with dark shadows jumping in the headlights.

When we arrived at the Santa Ana River, we followed Dad to the water's edge. He scouted the area looking for level ground and water devoid of anything that would eat our lines. When he found the perfect spot, he laid out a yellow and white checkered quilt and instructed us to sit on the blanket. "Now, be quiet, or you'll scare the fish!" Dad teased.

He approached me first and opened the rectangular green tackle box. Dad's rolled-up shirt sleeve exposed his hairy forearm and tattoo: the United States Marine Corps eagle, globe, and anchor emblem. A proud tribute and remembrance of the time he served in the Korean War. I spent many days running my finger around the outline of the black ink. To my eyes, the solemn eagle perched on top of the globe meant it was watching over the world. Protecting me. Like my dad.

"Here, reach into this cup and get a worm." Dad pushed the white foam container toward me.

"I don't see anything!"

He swept away the top layer of brown dirt with his finger, exposing disgusting wiggly red worms.

"Ew! I'm not picking that up!"

"Then it looks like you won't be fishing today!"

He stood up and ran his hand through his thick wavy black hair. Reaching into his shirt pocket, he pulled out his red pack of unfiltered Pall Mall cigarettes, lit one, took a long drag, and looked down at me. "You gonna change your mind before I ask your brave sisters?"

Not only was I unwilling to let my sisters upstage me, I knew the minute he walked away, I would be losing an opportunity for another minute with him. I was not going to let that happen.

"Alright, let me try!" I rallied the courage and grabbed a worm that didn't look as menacing as the others. I held it as far away from my body as possible while it squirmed, and I squealed.

Smiling, he said, "Atta girl! Now stick it on this hook!"

I cocked my head to look up at him. At 5'11", he loomed over me. "What do you mean?"

"Like this!" He demonstrated by threading the thrashing worm—expanding, contracting, and curling around his finger—through the point of the glistening hook. He had gone too far! Between the battered worm that I knew was dying a slow death and the intimidating barb that I knew I would stab myself with, I refused. "Alright, I'll do it this time, but someday you're going to have to learn how."

Dad baited the line, cast out, and told me to keep my eye on the red and white floater. "When it bobs up and down, yank up and reel it in," he instructed—another tough order for an eight-year-old when every water movement translated to a fish on the line. Between the four of us girls, there was a lot of reeling that day with nothing to show for it but an empty hook.

After an hour of tangled fishing lines and muddied girls slipping into the water, Dad decided it was time for a break. We sat cross-legged, sipping cocoa from our thermos lids while wisps of hot steam escaped into the oaks arched above us.

"Dad! Sing the first Marine!" Carole begged.

"Naw, I can't do that. The fish will laugh at me!"

Giggling, we all chimed in, "Come on, Daddy!"

With a smirk, he began:

"The first Marine he found a bean parlez vous,

"The second marine he cooked the bean parlez vous,

"The third marine he ate the bean and pooped all over the sub-marine [wherein he made a farting sound], inky dinky parlez vous."

We turned somersaults and laughed with pure joy. It was a good day.

⤙

Robert Gene Morris, tall, dark, and handsome, was the middle child of Angelo and Mollie Morris. His grandmother emigrated from Russia and his grandfather from Portugal—the Azores. Their native Portuguese surname, Mores, was changed to Morris somewhere along the line.

Dad's family was the polar opposite of our mother's. They were quiet and reserved, as opposed to the loud, animated Chicagoans. Religion was not central to their family. Dad baptized Lutheran, then converted to Catholicism when he married Mom. He dropped out of high school at seventeen to join the Marines and fight in the Korean War. Later in life, he was very proud of the GED he earned while working full time providing for the ten of us.

In 1950 when Mom and Dad married, they moved to Berkeley with our father's parents. Mom, pregnant with me, stayed home while Dad worked for a steel company as a welder. He was also a drummer with a country-western band.

After my birth, they returned to Fresno and lived in the projects—public housing for low-income and veterans. My father worked for Shepherd Rug company laying carpet...and my mother! Mom had a baby girl every year for four consecutive years.

I was a Daddy's girl. His pet name for me was KathiPat, which was a combination of my first and middle names. Quiet, gentle, and unassuming, if I did something to irritate my mother, I ran as fast as my little legs could muster and jumped onto his lap. My mother's glare did not affect me while under my dad's protection.

Nothing brought Dad more joy than performing for us and making us laugh. We couldn't get enough of his magic acts—making his thumb disappear or pulling pennies out of our ears. At the dinner table, he squished mashed potatoes through his teeth while Mom groaned, "Oh, Bob!" His trademark was to imitate an ape. While making a monkey face, he would pretend to hang from a tree with one hand and scratch his armpit with the other.

Dad relaxed by building miniature die-cast cars. Many nights I found him alone in the garage, absorbed with the models. One look at his laser-focused eyes *signaled do not disturb—genius at work.* Spread on his workbench were complicated instructions, a million parts, and vials of metallic paint in all colors of the rainbow.

With a steady hand and a cigarette hanging from his lips, he meticulously brushed the tiny doors and hoods with vibrant colors. Pungent turpentine blended with the cigarette smoke and spun in clouds above us. After the parts dried, he assembled them like a master craftsman with glue and a tiny screwdriver. Eager to show visitors his handiwork, he opened the doors, spun the tires, and turned the steering wheel. His smile was as radiant as the shiny candy apple red Studebaker and emerald green Packard. A dozen cars sat on a high shelf, elevated to a place of honor.

Building model cars and fishing were my father's only hobbies. He taught me glory in both.

᠊ᢣ᠊

In 1956, when Dad was twenty-seven years old, we moved two-hundred miles south from Fresno to Pacoima. That move turned out to be the best of our life. Dad landed a job with the Kinney Shoes Corporation. His first store was in Panorama City—a neighborhood in Los Angeles.

The manager of the store, Harold Rowen, was a machine and expected nothing less of his employees. My father, not one to shy away from demanding work, kept up with him and worked twelve-hour days, seven days a week. Their drive catapulted the store to the top of the leaderboard with the most sales in the entire company. It also advanced Dad to manager and Harold to the President and CEO of Kinney Shoes.

Dad had carved a name for himself with sales. It might have been an unfair advantage when he showed customers a photograph of us seven kids wearing Kinney Shoes. In the late 1950s, the minimum wage was one dollar. Kid's shoes averaged five dollars. His pitch was that outfitting seven children was expensive. He wanted his kids in quality shoes, and nothing was superior to Kinney's.

Kinney Shoes was expanding rapidly and needed a strong manager to open a new store in Garden Grove. Dad, disciplined and likable (with a proven track record), fit the bill. We moved for that store's grand opening. His performance garnered him another transfer six months later for another grand opening, and then another. For three years, we moved every six months throughout southern California to cities such as Lennox, Anaheim, and Inglewood for each new store's grand opening.

Kinney's became a way of life for our entire family. Mom occasionally worked part-time. She cashiered, sold handbags, nylons, and other accessories. After hours, we kids helped take inventory, sometimes late into the night. It was fun counting shoeboxes, running through the aisles, and climbing the shelving in the stock room.

Their company picnics were the best. Held annually in lush green parks with hundreds of happy employees and their families, it was old-fashioned fun. Children joined forces for burlap sack races, and adults squared off with three-legged competitions. Picnic tables, covered with red and white checkered tablecloths, held enough food to feed an army. We lined up for juicy hamburgers and hot dogs fresh off the grill with all the fixings and gorged on homemade vanilla ice cream and apple pie.

In June 1959, I had just completed second grade in Lennox when Dad was transferred again. We spent all day loading a moving truck, drove forty miles to a rental home in Orange, California, and unpacked. The goal to move everything in one day was derailed by seven of us kids coming down with the measles. As the day progressed, one by one, another kid broke out in red spots.

Our parents decided to spend the night at our new home and finish moving the following day. Early the next morning, we returned to the Lennox house and loaded the rest of our belongings. It was dark when we headed back to Orange. Dad drove the moving truck while all of us kids rode in the car with Mom.

As we got closer to the neighborhood, we saw towering flames and billowing black smoke. Mom started repeating, "God, please don't let it be our house." When we arrived at our street and turned the corner, we saw mayhem, four fire engines, and our house on fire. Firefighters with axes and hoses battled the blaze while people anxiously watched from their lawns.

Neighbors who saw us the previous day told the firefighters eight kids had moved into the house. Because children often hide under beds or in closets when there's a fire, the crew spent a lot of time looking for us. We were sad to learn that one fireman was injured in the search.

An exploding floor furnace in the living room caused the fire. The house was saved, but not without major damage. There were gaping holes in the roof, walls, and floor from the explosion and the firefighters cutting through the house.

We spent the night with a relative and returned the next morning to inspect the damage. The front lawn had our living room furniture strewn all over it. Everything was charred, melted, or destroyed. The wooden end tables, green upholstered armchairs, and a drum set. The sofa next to the heater was obliterated, with only remnants of the frame and portions of the yellow interior foam remaining.

Inside the house, the first thing I noticed was the smell—like a smoldering campfire, only different somehow. Everywhere I looked, the fire had left its mark. The varnish on the piano dripped down its legs. The plastic cover on the doorbell melted. Our clothes were drenched with water and soot and reeked with a wretched smell that permeated everything. The scene was unsettling to my young senses. To this day, I can see the images and remember the smell.

For the next several months, I lived separately from my parents. They stayed in hotels with my younger siblings while we older girls rotated among Mom's friends. I was eight and had no idea why we had to live apart; I just knew I hated every minute of it. Especially when I had to sleep with a girl my age who still wet the bed. It was bad enough that I couldn't fall asleep, but waking up saturated in her pee was repulsive.

I cried when Mom visited, explained my horrible situation, and begged her to take me with her. Her response was to say the Rosary because it would help me fall asleep. I tried her method, sometimes saying the Rosary multiple times in one night. It didn't help, but I'm confident the number of prayers said during those months has carried me through my lifetime.

We ended that year celebrating Christmas in a motel room. Our exhilaration and excitement of being together multiplied when we walked into the room. A decorated two-foot artificial tree sat on the dresser. Mesh stockings filled with candy and toys hung from the bedposts. But nothing compared to us being together—our parents and eight kids huddled together on two beds and the floor.

On Christmas morning, we received our greatest gift. Our parents announced we were staying together! Dad had been transferred to northern California.

⤳

We moved to Stockton and bought our first home. We had to sell it a year later when Kinney's transferred our father to Vallejo. The following year, when he was asked to move to San Jose, Dad agreed…but put his foot down and said it would be the last time he would move.

I was eleven when we moved to San Jose. I'd lived in eleven cities, eleven homes, and attended nine different schools. Always the new girl in class and the new kid on the block, I thought everyone lived as we did. When we moved to San Jose, I was surprised to learn that most of my sixth-grade classmates had grown up with each other.

We lived in San Jose for two years, and for most of that time, our parents had stopped going to church. They dropped us off at Mass and we walked home. Once, after receiving communion at the altar, I passed out, and an adult had to call our parents to pick us up.

Back home, I confronted my mother.

"Mom! Why are you making us go to church? You and Dad don't go!"

"I'm not going because I am mad at God," she replied indignantly.

"For what?"

"For burning our house down."

"Oh, brother! God didn't burn our house down! The heater exploded!"

The following Sunday, she and Dad went to church.

I loved everything about San Jose—the weather, the people, and my school. Dad loved it too. He managed the Kinney's Shoe store in Saratoga and gifted himself with a mynah bird. His crowning moment was when he taught it to say, "Birds don't talk." He kept it in a high corner of the store and enjoyed showing it off to his customers.

All was well with the world until the wee hours of a night in 1964—a night that left our father emotionally bankrupt. The Saratoga Kinney Shoe store caught fire. The next morning, when we drove into the parking lot and saw the skeletal remains sprawled in front of us,

Mom and I gasped. I looked to my dad for a reaction. He looked like a ghost—all color had drained from his face.

The red brick that framed the front and sides of the building was charred black. The roof had collapsed. The storefront glass lay shattered on the pavement. We parked and made our way inside. It looked like a war zone with ankle-deep debris strewn everywhere—burned chairs, shoes, and handbags. Twisted, melted shelving in the stock room had fallen like Pick-Up Sticks. Piles of burnt shoeboxes. The fire destroyed everything.

The familiar wretched stench reminded me of the day our home burned four years earlier. The standout difference was that we had spent one night in the house. It held no memories. Kinney Shoes held infinite memories. Dad's entire life lay sprawled before him in a pool of black ash.

The investigation could not determine the source of the fire, so Kinney's blamed my dad and fired him. They accused him of setting the store ablaze because of low sales. Their allegations were ludicrous and baseless to anyone that knew my father. Dad had devoted his life to Kinney Shoes. His value system and work ethics were impeccable. If Dad had done it, he surely would have removed his beloved pet— the mynah bird was found charred in its cage.

To lose his career devastated him. He gave eight years of his life to Kinney's and moved us around like Army brats. Unemployed, with a wife and nine children, the stress affected my father's health. He suffered from stomach issues for most of his adult life and had been admitted to the hospital twice for a bleeding ulcer.

Shortly after the incident, my parents went out with friends while I babysat. We were all asleep when they returned at 2:00 a.m. I awoke to my mother yelling, "I don't feel sorry for you! That's what you get for drinking!"

"Joyce, I'm vomiting blood!" Dad sounded terrified.

I began to cry—loud enough for my mother to hear me. Mom came into my bedroom and whispered, "Kathi, I thought you were sleeping. Why are you crying?" Her calm and soothing voice was in stark contrast to her screams at my dad.

"I can hear Daddy. Is he going to die?"

"No, he's fine. He just had too much to drink."

"I'm scared. I think you should take him to the hospital!"

"Don't worry about your dad. He'll be fine in the morning. Now go to sleep."

I eventually dozed off with the ever-present fear that one day I would find Dad dead in a pool of blood.

～

Dad found employment with a bakery. He drove a van through neighborhoods selling bread, donuts, and other pastries. It was a significant pay cut, so to help financially, Mom worked at a dry cleaner. That lasted a couple of months before Mom got pregnant with her tenth child.

Mom knew she would be unable to work the entire nine months, and Dad still wanted to manage a shoe store. Grandma convinced them to return to Fresno, where we would be close to family. My father applied for a management position with a shoe store in downtown Fresno and got hired. We left for Fresno just in time for me to start eighth grade.

⌣

Most of Mom's family lived in Fresno, as did Dad's sister, Aunt Eleanor. For most of our lives, there was distance between our father's side of the family and us—physically and figuratively. Most of them lived in the Bay Area while we moved around the state. I cannot recall one holiday, vacation, or birthday with Dad's family. Indifference may have kept us apart, rather than bad blood. I honestly don't know. But when Aunt Eleanor invited us to her home for a Christmas party, my parents eagerly accepted. She also invited Aunt Glo—Dad's oldest sister.

That Christmas, our father splurged on a special gift for Mom and wanted to share his shining moment with his sisters. He had the giant box professionally wrapped in regal forest green paper, tied with an enormous gold bow. The night of the party, he paced the house like a caged animal. When everyone settled in the living room, Dad stood and announced, "Joyce, this year has been rough, so I wanted to buy something special for you."

"OK, Bob, but why are you giving it to me now?" Our tradition was to open gifts on Christmas morning.

"Because I think you can use it tonight!" Mom, seven months pregnant, joined Dad at the front of the living room. He handed her the beautifully wrapped package.

My mother beamed as she carefully unwrapped the box and burst into tears when she saw its contents. My mother joked for years that she wanted a chinchilla fur coat. Beneath the gold tissue paper was a faux mink. It may not have been an expensive fur, but from the look on her face, I knew its value was far greater. That box held my father's beating heart.

With tears streaming down her face, she kissed Dad and stroked the fur as he helped her put it on. When she turned to show us, Aunt Glo muttered, "She looks like a bear!"

My mother ran down the hallway, sobbing. Dad tried to console her, but the damage was done. From that day forward, my mother had a great disdain for Aunt Glo, which is a nicer way of saying she hated her. When Aunt Glo fought for custody of us, the thought ever-present in my mind was *if Mom knew her children were awarded to Aunt Glo, she would roll over in her grave.*

⤳

Dad worked in Fresno for a year before finding his final job in Madera, managing Kaser Shoes. He worked there for three years and made many friends, including the police who patrolled downtown. He loved practical jokes and enlisted a police officer's help to play one on our mother. Dad worked late one night and called Mom.

"Joyce, I need you to pick me up."

"Why aren't one of your employees giving you a ride home?"

"They left a long time ago. I stayed late to dye some shoes."

"Bob, I am not coming to get you. I've got curlers in my hair! You can walk home!"

"It will take you five minutes. Just pull into the alley, and I will meet you outside."

"Alright, but you better be ready and waiting."

Mom always took the same route beginning on the main street, Yosemite. She drove a short distance when a black and white, Dad's partner in crime, turned on its flashing lights and siren. Mom pulled over. The police officer walked to her window.

"Good evening, ma'am. I need your driver's license and registration."

Mom fumbled for her license, handed it to him, and asked, "I'm sorry, officer, but can you please tell me why you pulled me over?"

"Well, ma'am, it's a crime going out in public looking like that!"

⌁

We moved to Madera when I was fourteen and beginning my freshman year in high school. My parents kept a tight rein. Dad lectured me on the virtues of being a virgin and explained what teenage boys really want from a girl. I wasn't allowed to date until I turned sixteen and forbidden to ride in cars with boys. Their rules were frustrating when it seemed like everyone else had boyfriends and went places, so I decided to push for freedom when I turned seventeen.

I begged to go to the school dances. My argument was they were held in the gymnasium or local halls and supervised—so what could I do wrong? To my surprise, they agreed I could go but insisted on dropping me off and picking me up. I had a blast dancing and hanging out with friends. When the clock struck midnight, my parents were waiting outside.

All was well until the night Lenny, a guy I had been insanely infatuated with for three years, asked me to slow dance. He smelled good and looked even better. All rules, lectures, and common sense disappeared when he pulled me close and looked at me with his deep brown eyes. Wrapped in the dream of a young girl's fantasy, I was his to lead astray. We left the dance, drove to his house, and made out in the front seat of his car. He took me back to the hall before midnight.

When the dance ended, I left the building, my parents pulled up, and off we went. It was too easy—I had gotten away with my lark!

In the following weeks, I successfully left a couple more dances. My grave mistake was to brag to my sisters, who, unbeknownst to me, told my parents.

At the next dance, my parents arrived an hour early to pick me up. They parked across the street and waited. I had left that night with the brother of my infatuation. He and I drove to an orchard, sat under the orange trees, and talked more than anything else. We left at 11:30 p.m. and headed back to the hall. He pulled his black coupe into the parking lot, and together we walked into the building.

When I exited at midnight, I spotted my parents waiting across the street. I sprinted to them and opened the car door. When I climbed into the back seat, Mom asked, "So how was the dance, Kathi?"

"It was great!" I responded with enthusiasm

"Did you have fun?" Dad asked.

"Yeah, all my friends were there!"

"Like who?" Mom's words were terse. It was my first clue something was amiss.

"Pat, Judy, Susan, a lot of my girlfriends."

"Did you leave the dance?" Dad asked, gritting his teeth.

"No. Why would I do that?" I knew I was busted.

Our home was down the street, just minutes from the hall. By the time we parked, my father was out of control. To see him that angry was out of character and alarming—I wasn't sure what he might do. I raced to my bedroom and tried to escape into the closet. He grabbed my long hair and pulled me out, slapped me, and said, "You're a liar! We were parked across the street and saw you get out of a car!"

To get him to stop pulling my hair, I yelled, "I hate you! Let go of my hair!"

With that lie, he let go and said, "I know you do."

With his response, I died a thousand deaths.

He left crying and walked for an hour through our dark neighborhood. He didn't speak to me for the following two weeks…the whole two weeks before the night he was killed.

The last memory I have with my dad is me saying *I hate you.* I didn't get the opportunity to say I'm sorry. I didn't get the chance to say I lied. Not one second of my entire life did I hate him.

The dance hall I left the night of our fight was VFW—Veterans of Foreign Wars. Corporal Robert Morris, my dad, my hero, was protecting his KathiPat.

I'm sorry, Dad.

I love you with everything in me.

I always did.

I always will.

Dad, Marine, served Jan. 9, 1947 to Jan. 8, 1950 and fought in the Korean War

Dad, 1, 1930

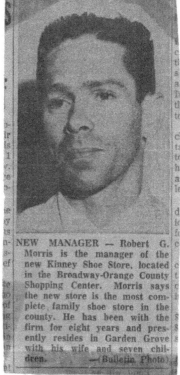

NEW MANAGER — Robert G. Morris is the manager of the new Kinney Shoe Store, located in the Broadway-Orange County Shopping Center. Morris says the new store is the most complete, family shoe store in the county. He has been with the firm for eight years and presently resides in Garden Grove with his wife and seven children. —(Bulletin Photo)

Dad, Manager for Kinney Shoes,
Garden Grove, 1958

Mom, 24, and Dad, 28, Kinney
Shoes, Garden Grove, 1957

Chapter 32

THE DRUNK DRIVER

Clifford Salmon's blood alcohol content was 0.19 percent and he was driving on a revoked license when he killed my parents. He was booked into the Fresno County jail and bail was set at $5,000. He was released on July 18, 1968, after posting $1,250. A month later, while awaiting trial, Salmon was arrested in Porterville and sentenced to ten days in jail for public intoxication and violating probation.

His record included nine misdemeanor drunk driving convictions, a misdemeanor hit and run violation, a reckless driving violation, several public intoxication charges, and several convictions for driving with a revoked license.

In September 1968 he pled innocent to two counts of felony manslaughter and one count of felony drunk driving. On November 22, 1968, he pled guilty to two counts of felony manslaughter and was sentenced to one to five years in state prison—the California Medical Facility at Vacaville, California. The felony drunk driving charge was dismissed "in the interest of justice."

Uncle Gene filed a $500,000 civil lawsuit charging negligence against Salmon. The suit also named Audrey Crowe—the woman that sold him his car. Because the title to the vehicle had not been transferred, Crowe's insurance paid $30,000. After lawyer's fees, each of us received around $2,000. Salmon had no assets, so he paid nothing.

As strange as it seems, I never thought about the drunk driver. I was a young and naïve seventeen-year-old in the spotlight. I was struggling with how to survive without parents, the fame, the legal system, the relatives, the foster homes, becoming an adult alone in the world and a single mother, and panic attacks. I had no emotional space left to think about him too. Someone asked me the first week after the accident what I thought about the man that killed my parents. I responded that he would feel bad when he sobered up and realized that he orphaned ten kids. However, even though we were national news and easy to contact, he never reached out. Someone that felt remorse would have apologized.

I didn't get angry until fifty years later while researching to write about him. When I discovered that he was seventy-one years old when he died, I became infuriated. That day my life without my mom and dad flashed before me like a movie reel. High school graduations, birthdays, weddings, vacations, and holidays. I thought about my son and how he would have enjoyed his grandfather's sense of humor and love for the outdoors. I thought about my daughter and how she would have bonded with my mother better than I had. The more I reflected on how he robbed me and my family of a lifetime of experiences, the more inflamed I became until I was screaming like a raging maniac.

And then I let it go. I chose to move on.

Anger is not going to change a thing but steal my peace.

I refuse to give him that power.

Chapter 33

AGORAPHOBIA

Growing up, I was a free spirit with no fear. However, five years after the death of my parents, I had a panic attack. It came unexpectedly while watching television. As the weeks progressed, I began having panic attacks all day, every day.

The anxiety was like nothing I had ever experienced. My nerves were like live wires where I would jump at the slightest sound or provocation. I couldn't focus on anything but the physical feelings that I was experiencing. I went to a psychiatrist who told me that because I had not properly grieved the death of my parents, the trauma manifested itself physically. His solution was pills. He prescribed Sinequan, which made me extremely lethargic, so I refused to take it and stopped seeing him. I wanted help. Not a pill that turned me into a zombie.

My life was hell for over fifteen years. My world closed in. Home became my safe haven. I couldn't drive more than five miles from my house without having a panic attack. I stopped riding with others because I didn't want to have to explain why they needed to take me home. Public transportation was out of the question because I was not in control. And as the weeks rolled on, so did my confinement. I couldn't go anywhere without having a panic attack: grocery store, movie theater, drive-through for fast food. I didn't have a honeymoon, and we didn't take family vacations.

The entire world was scary. My life centered around "what ifs." What if I am going insane? What if this panic attack never stops? What if I have a brain tumor? What if I have a heart attack? What if I pass out? What if I get a flat tire? What if I can't get out of the parking lot fast enough? What if I get stuck in the elevator? The list was endless. And with each what if, my anxiety and panic escalated. Like a tiger chasing its tail building up more and more speed. Or a deer with its antlers stuck in a tree, thrashing about, and going nowhere. The fear of a panic attack created a self-made prison. I didn't know how to deal with it, and I didn't understand what my problem was.

Then one day by happenstance a program on television talked about the granddaddy of phobias—agoraphobia. When a psychiatrist explained the symptoms, I began sobbing because he was describing me to a T. It was liberating to know that my condition had a name, I wasn't insane, and I wasn't the only one suffering from it.

The following definition is from Wikipedia:

> "Agoraphobia is an anxiety disorder characterized by symptoms of anxiety in situations where the person perceives their environment to be unsafe with no easy way to escape. These situations can include open spaces, public transit, shopping centers, or simply being outside their home. Being in these situations may result in a panic attack. The symptoms

occur nearly every time the situation is encountered and last for more than six months. Those affected will go to great lengths to avoid these situations. In severe cases people may become completely unable to leave their homes. Agoraphobia is believed to be due to a combination of genetic and environmental factors. The condition often runs in families, and stressful or traumatic events such as the death of a parent or being attacked may be a trigger."

Shortly after watching that program, I found TERRAP (acronym for territorial apprehension). It is a comprehensive treatment program, including cognitive behavioral therapy, desensitization methods, education, and support for the panic sufferer and their family. I had group therapy for many weeks. Listening to others on how agoraphobia affected them and knowing that I was not alone was a tremendous relief in itself. The program helped with coping skills; however, I still struggled with traveling distances. So, when I turned thirty-five, I found a psychologist who taught me relaxation techniques. He challenged me to drive increasingly further distances. Each victory gave me the courage to push the boundaries until I was able to drive four hundred miles from home.

I also strengthened my walk with God and leaned into my faith. I went to Mass and read the Bible. I also joined prayer groups. It brought me comfort to have others pray over me and for me.

I learned that when life throws a curve ball, it is critical to have a genuine relationship with God to survive. Early on, when my relationship was nonexistent or weak, I struggled. As my faith grew stronger, and I was dealt another blow, I was better equipped to handle it.

While writing, it became crystal clear that the reason I've made it this far is because God met me at every abyss.

It took years of therapy, courage, and faith to feel normal again. I am no longer plagued by daily panic attacks, but still suffer with what I call residual agoraphobia. I still have the ability to work myself up to a full-blown panic attack on rare occasions. The difference today is that I know the physical symptoms are not life-threatening—it's an adrenaline rush—and that I have the tools to get through it. Tools like deep breathing, self-talk, or just letting go and riding the wave of panic till it subsides. Therapy and God taught me that.

For all those whose lives have been impacted by a drunk driver, my wish is that my story gives you hope. I am seventy years old. I survived, and for the most part, I am happy. I can't promise that it will be easy. I realized that if I didn't get it together, I would be left behind because the world was not stopping for my pain. I decided to do whatever it took to pull myself up and keep going: God, therapy, and self-help books. I cried, screamed, wrote how I felt, and talked to whoever would listen. Little by little I improved.

The best analogy a therapist gave me when I was struggling with panic attacks, anxiety, and depression was to compare it to a bouncing ball. In the beginning the highs are extremely high and the lows are extremely low. But as the months roll on the highs are not as high and the lows are not as low. Until one day the ball has no bounce left in it.

When all else failed, I visualized myself curled up in the palm of God's hand and believed that He would not allow anything to harm me.

That's faith.

Chapter 34

TRUST FUND
LETTERS AND FINAL
DISBURSEMENT

For many years after the accident, Madera held nothing but nightmarish memories. I couldn't drive past that town without suffering crippling panic attacks that brought me to my knees. For that reason, ten and a half years passed before I thought about the letters sent to us from around the world. I wondered if the bank still had them. Emotionally I was in a better mindset where I could more fully appreciate everyone's condolences. I wanted to read them and ideally find a way to show my gratitude, but I had to face my fear of driving to Madera.

Was I strong enough? Would I fall apart? I wasn't sure how I would react, but it was a risk I was willing to take. I felt it essential for my healing to go through the rite of passage. So, in 1979 I made my daring trek to the Bank of America in Madera.

When I entered the bank and stepped up to the teller, she recognized me instantly. I used to babysit her daughters. After exchanging niceties, I explained that I was there to pick up the letters and hoped they still had them. She excused herself to ask her manager. When she returned, her first words were, "I am so sorry." My heart sank. She went on to explain that their record retention was ten years. "It's been ten and a half years, so the letters were destroyed six months ago. The stacks of boxes were taking up valuable space, so we had no choice."

Why didn't someone try to contact us? The trustees included Bank of America—they had our contact information. From the thousands of letters sent from throughout the United States, the soldiers in Vietnam, and people in foreign counties, all I have are a handful of empty envelopes and a few letters.

⁓

The foster homes received social security benefits to support us. The primary purpose of the trust fund was for our education; however, foster homes petitioned the trust fund for other expenses. To illustrate how the trust fund was drained, Aunt Mary, who fostered Eddie in 1979, petitioned for the following that year: clothing $425, car repairs $144, bicycle $135, major medical expenses $154, dental expenses $100, medical and medicine $300, fall tuition $880, and unforeseen expenses $1,000—a total of $3,138. One of the foster homes petitioned for a station wagon, and when my siblings were removed from their house, they gave the car to Aunt Mary since Eddie had been placed with her. After she threw him out like trash, she sold the car and kept the profit.

For all the good intentions behind the trust fund, it failed miserably. At a time when we craved love and emotional support from adults, money prevailed. As the account increased, disinterested relatives suddenly took an interest. As time marched on, foster care that appeared to the outside world as selfless was in truth self-serving.

The trust fund was dispersed on September 8, 1983. For losing both our parents, the ten of us each received a check for $7,709.

Chapter 35

EPILOGUE

On July 2, 1968, our lives were altered forever. We were exemplary kids with morals, character, and integrity until placed into the foster care system—where they take hurt children and hurt them some more. Despite national publicity we were treated no different than the next fostered child aching for a loving and nurturing home and receiving the complete opposite.

Adults should never have asked ten traumatized kids where they wanted to live. I know that having the spotlight on us put added pressure on our relatives and the authorities. But, in the end, more harm than good was done.

My opinion on where to place us should have carried the least weight. I was less than a year shy of turning eighteen. Eddie, the three-year-old, should have been the primary focus. Ten children are a lot to ask of anyone, so I believe we should have been placed with someone with a track record. Surely, in those thousands of offers to adopt was a

Catholic couple who had adopted before. The social workers, instead of interviewing us on where we wanted to live, should have selected a couple who had adopted children and interviewed their adopted children, to determine if the couple was loving and nurturing.

Michael chose to end his pain. Others of us that went wayward eventually found our way back and stood on the foundation that our parents instilled in us—impeccable work ethics and responsibility. We overcame challenges and had successful careers.

Our journey is too distressing for my siblings to relive. Scarred with unimaginable trauma and unresolved grief, digging up the past brings emotional pain and anger. They value their privacy and have chosen to live their lives quietly. They have a right to protect themselves and move on from what harmed us so profoundly.

Contrary to what many believe, writing did not feel therapeutic. It gutted me. Opening Pandora's box to write about my experiences was brutal. I sobbed over losing my parents, my siblings, and my brothers. I screamed at the drunk that killed my parents. I wept for my younger self and how I felt disposable by everyone. I cried imagining how Mom and Dad would have felt knowing their children were mistreated, abused, and discarded. I ached for what could have been.

But I got through it like I always do. I learned long ago that I won't cry forever, life goes on with or without me, and when it feels like I am holding on by a thread, this, too, shall pass.

Everyone that read the paper or saw us on the news thought we rode into the sunset to live happily ever after with our aunt and a lot of money. Nothing could have been further from the truth. But we rose from the ashes clinging to each other. For that I am grateful.

I want to end by thanking everyone that supported us in our time of need. Our family is deeply grateful. I will never know who all of you are, but God knows. And that's what matters most.

On behalf of the Morris family:

Bob, Joyce, Kathi, Judy, Linda, Carole, Theresa, Roberta, Robert, Mike, Jeff, and Ed

Thank you!

Exodus 22:22

"You shall not mistreat any widow or fatherless child. If you do mistreat them, and they cry out to me, I will surely hear their cry, and my wrath will burn, and I will kill you with the sword, and your wives shall become widows and your children fatherless."

Acknowledgments

First and foremost, I want to thank God for calling me to write this memoir and carrying me through the long, arduous, and painful task of bringing it to completion. And Monsignor Perry Kavookjian, God's conduit and my dear friend, whose inspiring sermon was the catalyst for this book.

I have many people to thank, living and deceased, beginning with Patrick O'Rourke (RIP), the photographer for the *Madera Tribune*. He was my first contact when I began the book and the first to encourage me.

I want to thank my neighbors, Ray and Marge (RIP) McKnight, that allowed me to hunker down in their Bay Area condo in 2009 where I pounded out chapter one. I held my breath as Marge, who had earned a Master's degree in English, and Ray, a Harvard graduate and retired English professor, read the pages and felt relieved when they both gave me, a college dropout, a thumbs up.

I want to thank my Writing for Publication Class led by Janice Stevens and all my classmates. Your critiques and support championed me to the finish line. I found my tribe the day I stepped into class and for that I am forever grateful. Each and every one of you hold a special place in my heart, but none more than CJ Collins—may she rest in peace. CJ, as my developmental editor, lives in these pages. Our goal was to party like rock stars when my book published, but cancer had other ideas. She will live on in the hearts of many and I will forever cherish our short four years.

A special shout out to Clarice Krikorian—the first to read my pages from start to finish. Your kindness will not be forgotten.

I want to thank my family, friends, and Facebook friends who patiently waited years and cheered me on every step of the way. Thank you for your support and for seeing value in my story when I couldn't.

Special thanks to Bonnie Hearn Hill and Hazel Dixon-Cooper for leading me to Post Hill Press. It was an incredible gift that I can never repay.

To Anthony Ziccardi, thank you for taking a chance on me. I am forever indebted to you and your wonderful team including Maddie Sturgeon, Devon Brown, Rachel Hoge, and Kiera Baron.

To my heart and soul and reason for living: my children Cherise and Ryan; grandchildren Kylie, Marcus, Jonathan, Ryan Jr., and Christian; and my great-granddaughters Ma'Kyia and Dior—thank you for your constant love despite my phobias and shortcomings. It's a wonderful world because you are my sunshine, my hemoglobin, and the Piglet to my Pooh. I love you all to the moon, back to your hearts, to infinity, and more.

To my parents Robert Gene and Joyce Angela Morris, thank you for giving birth to a legacy—your ten children. Thank you for instilling in us strong core values of integrity, morals, and an unfaltering love for God. There is no denying that the foundation you laid carried us through our worst nightmare—losing you.

Most of all, to my brothers and sisters: I love you Judy, Linda, Carole, Theresa, Roberta, Robert, Mike, Jeff, and Eddie. We are a club unto ourselves—one that nobody would willingly pay the ultimate price to join.

Mom, 17, and Dad, 21, on their wedding day in Reno, July 17, 1950

Last photo of Mom and Dad taken one month before they were killed.
Carole's 8th grade graduation, Madera, California, June, 1968

Calvary Cemetery, Madera, California

The last photo of Mom and Dad with all of us, taken three years
before Eddie was born. San Jose, California, 1962

Front, left to right: Robert, Roberta, Jeff (on Mom's lap), Mom, Dad,
Theresa, Mike Back, left to right: Linda, Kathi, Judy, Carole

Madera Tribune, Aug. 6, 1968, by Pat O'Rourke; Kathi, 17

Madera Tribune, Aug. 6, 1968, by Pat O'Rourke; Judy, 16, drawing Carole, 14

Madera Tribune, Aug. 6, 1968, by Pat O'Rourke; Roberta, 11, Linda, 15

Madera Tribune, Aug. 6, 1968, by Pat O'Rourke; Theresa, 12

Madera Tribune, Aug. 6, 1968, by Pat O'Rourke; Roberta, 11, Eddie, 3, in front of our home in Madera where we were living when our parents were killed

Madera Tribune, Aug. 6, 1968, by Pat O'Rourke; Jeff, 8, Robert, 11, Mike, 10

Photo by Pat O'Rourke, July 1968.

Front, left to right: Linda, Jeff, Kathi with Eddie on her lap, Theresa, Mike

Back, left to right: Roberta, Judy, Grandma Lachawicz,
Carole, Robert, Father Bentivegna

Last photo taken of the ten of us in 1988.
Front, left to right: Roberta, Carole, Kathi, Linda
Middle, left to right: Ed, Theresa, Judy, Mike
Back, left to right: Jeff, Robert

About the Author

Photo by Heidi Jones Photography

Kathi Morris is the oldest of the ten Morris orphans and currently lives in Clovis, California. This memoir was a finalist in the 2019 San Francisco Writers Conference. She won grand prize at the iconic Sardine Factory in Monterey, California, where the movie *Play Misty for Me* was filmed, for her written tribute on their fiftieth anniversary commemoration. After a thirty-five-year career with the IRS, surviving divorce and ovarian cancer, she retired and worked for Pebble Beach Resorts. Her greatest joys are her children and grand-children, and her dream is to own a home in Monterey Bay.